# *A Radical Reformation of Neoclassical Economics*

## *Market Equilibrium, Perfect Competition, Value Theory, Income Distribution, Social Welfare*

Dimitrios Nomidis

**CIP a Camerei Naţionale a Cărţii**

**Nomidis, Dimitrios.**

A Radical Reformation of Neoclassical Economics : Market Equilibrium, Perfect Competition, Value Theory, Income Distribution, Social Welfare / Dimitrios Nomidis. – Generis Publishing, 2020 (Print on demand). – 71 p.: fig.

Rez.: lb. engl. – Referinţe bibliogr.: p. 59-60 şi în subsol.

ISBN 978-9975-153-39-3.

330.8

N 84

Cover image: Dimitrios Nomidis

Generis Publishing
Online orders: www.generis-publishing.com
Orders by email: info@generis-publishing.com

# Table of Contents

**Abstract**

During the second half of the twentieth century economic theory moved increasingly away from price theory, which was gradually displaced by more modern trends such as game theory, behavioral-empirical-experimental economics, neuroeconomics, heterodox economics, etc. This was due to serious shortcomings and mistakes of the traditional theory that is based on Neoclassical economics. The correction of those mistakes entails dramatic changes in the Neoclassical theory and its fundamental outcomes, concerning perfect competition, price determination, value theory, income distribution, social welfare, and other major fields of economics. This also results in an integrated theory in which market functions, regardless of the number of firms, i.e. from monopoly to perfect competition. Moreover, by this reformation traditional price theory regains its self-efficiency, prestige, and dominant position in economics.

## 1. Introduction

This book constitutes the synthesis of two previous working papers of the author (Nomidis 2015a, 2016a) in a way that they are integrated, improved and fitted, completing each other in order to present the complete view of the new revised theory.

Firstly in Section 1, it is demonstrated and proved that the concept of the neoclassical theory about price taking, i.e. perfectly elastic (horizontal) individual demand curve for the firms, is wrong and that the real individual demand curves are sloping and distribute evenly the total demand among the (like) firms at any price, thus summing up to the total demand curve (see Figure 4), which does not hold in the conventional theory although it should. The paper also attempts to trace historically this fallacy and detect the root causes that presumably led to it (Appendix A).

The correction of the above wrong approach and the adoption of the appropriate sloped demand curve for the firm entails a total and dramatic revision of the standard theory of Value, Perfect Competition and the associated theory of Social Welfare, since it invalidates the famous principle of price determination at intersection of total demand and total supply, as well as that of the equality of price to the minimum average cost in the long run, facts that move social welfare away from its maximum claimed by the neoclassical theory; in addition, in the labor market, labor is not paid according to the value of its marginal product, as neoclassicals argue, but according to the marginal product revenue, which implies the monopolistic exploitation of labor and lowers wage and employment levels, and in fact worsens the previous social welfare's loss.

The new theory covers in a single and integrated manner all types of market, from monopoly and duopoly to perfect competition, and demonstrates the unavoidably monopolistic nature of the market, even under perfect competition: The aggregate profit of the  industry equals the profit coming from a monopolistic exploitation of the market and is equally distributed among the like firms, until in perfect competition the revenue just covers the cost of the firm, thus leading to zero <u>economic</u> (i.e. extra) profit; this zero-profit stability happens due to the entry of new firms attracted by the extra profit, but also due to loss if a firm varied its production (since equilibrium takes place at the tangency point of demand and cost curves and any variation from this point would make price less than cost). This is the real reason for the stability of price in perfect competition and not the large number of tiny firms unable to affect the price and the falsely subsequent horizontal demand curve for the firms; those presumptions are not valid and have to be retired and the emphasis in perfect competition must be placed on the zero economic profit and the entry-exit of firms.

Section 2 of the paper demonstrates why the horizontal demand curve for the firms is false; Section 3 reveals what the real individual demand curves for the firms are; Section 4 demonstrates the monopolistic character of the market even under perfect competition; Section 5 presents the implications of the new reformed theory on economics and especially on the theories of Value, Perfect Competition and Social Welfare; Section 6 makes a summary and Section 7 concludes. Appendix A attempts to trace the fallacy of the traditional theory around the horizontal demand curve for the individual firm; Appendix B examines how the new approach works in the determination of equilibrium both at firm and at market level, and Appendix C provides mathematical validations for the wrong determination of price by the traditional theory at the intersection of total demand and total supply, and for the equilibrium and price determination according to the new theory.

## 2. The Fallacy of the Neoclassical Theory

Traditionally, the neoclassical theory of Perfect Competition builds its conclusions on the assumption that the individual demand curve for the product of each producer is perfectly elastic (horizontal) at the price determined by the intersection of the total Supply and total Demand of the produced commodity (price taking concept). This assumption is based on the argument that each producer can sell all of his production at the above market equilibrium price (even after an increase -however big- in his relatively small production compared to the total one) and that if a producer set a higher price he would sell nothing, while a lower price would bring about an unreasonable loss of revenue.

The above assumption, as well as its justification, is wrong leading to erroneous results and to inconsistencies in the theory itself. The basic arguments for this are presented below.

- Neoclassical theory sets as a presupposition that each entrepreneur maximizes their profit. Since this occurs at individual firm level, it can be mathematically proved[1] that it must also happen at the aggregate level. This means that, just as at firm level the equilibrium price and quantity are determined by the intersection of the marginal revenue with the marginal cost (for maximization of the profit), in the same way at aggregate market level the equilibrium price and quantity must be determined by the intersection of the total (aggregated) marginal revenue with the total (aggregated) marginal cost, and this equilibrium state also maximizes the profits of the industry as a whole. The aggregate marginal revenue, which is the horizontal sum of the firms' marginal revenues, equals the marginal revenue that comes from the total demand curve, while the aggregate marginal cost, which is the horizontal sum of the firms' marginal costs (=sum of the individual supplies), gives the market total supply curve[2]. **Thus the market equilibrium, which, must be noted, maximizes the profits of the whole industry, is determined by the intersection of the total supply with the marginal revenue of the total demand curve and not with the**

---

[1] See Appendix C: Mathematical Validation (Section C.1)

[2] As usual it is considered, for simplicity, that the production factors' prices, which affect the production cost, remain constant with the increased usage of the production factors from the firm level to the market level.

**total demand curve itself as argued by the neoclassical theory.** That is, in neoclassical theory the market equilibrium does not maximize the aggregate profit of the industry as a whole derived from the total market demand, while it should, which proves that it is wrong. This inconsistency of the neoclassical theory comes from the assumption about horizontal individual demand curve for the firms, which is wrong, while it is lifted with sloping individual demand curves summing up to the total demand.

• We should not forget that the total demand in the market consists of the sum of individual consumer demands and that this sum at a local level forms the demand for each firm and therefore these two demand curves must have the same form, since both of them reflect the consumer choices and demands just at different quantity levels. Therefore, the individual demand curve for the firm must have a form analogous to that of the total demand curve, reflecting just smaller quantities for same prices. If the individual demand curve for the firm were perfectly elastic (horizontal), how would it be possible for the total demand curve of the market, which is their sum, to have the normal form of a demand curve with a negative slope?

• As it is analyzed in the Appendix A of this book entitled "The Fallacy around the Horizontal Demand Curve for the Firm", this fallacy has been most probably developed from a misunderstood interpretation of a Cournot's (1838) phrase in his "Unlimited Competition" chapter of his infamous book "Mathematical Principles of the Theory of Wealth". The original meaning of that phrase was to denote the stability of equilibrium price in perfect competition, where the number of firms is very large and thus the production of each very small and unable to affect the prevalent price (see <u>Figure 1</u>). This was misinterpreted as horizontal demand curve for the individual firm's production, because, according to this phrase, a firm can vary its production as much as it wants (always small in relation to the total demand) and sell at the equilibrium price already determined in the market (before the variation in its individual production) without affecting this equilibrium price (Figure 1).

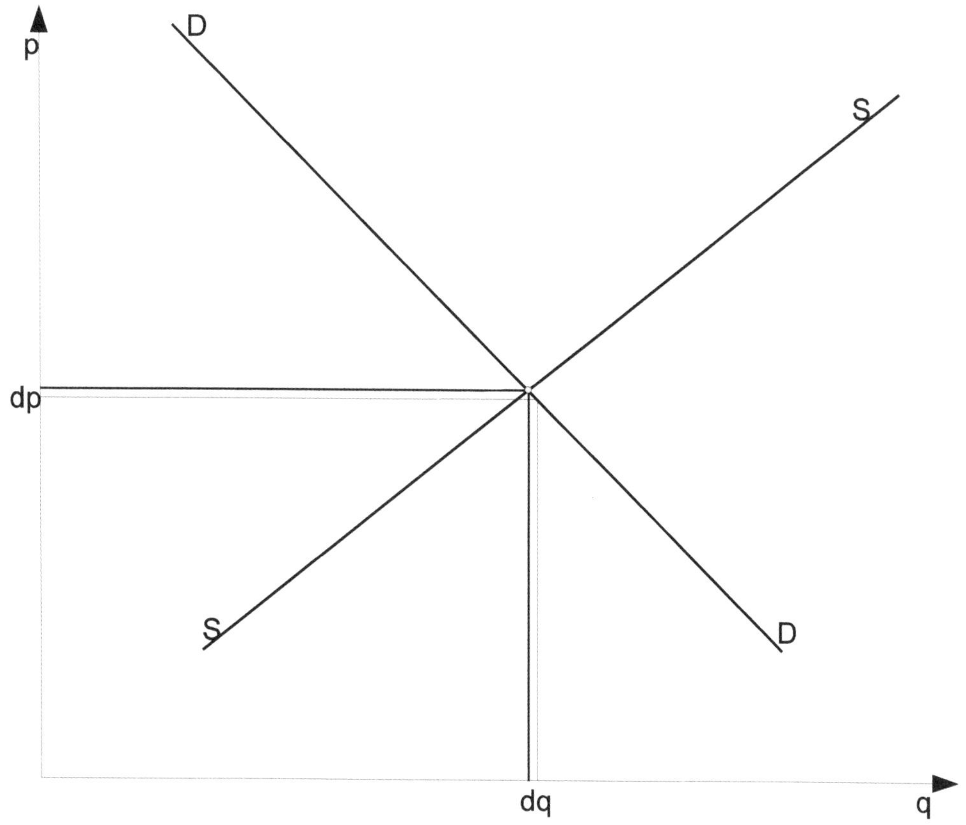


**FIGURE 1**

**The Classic Condition for Equilibrium Stability**

Because of the large number of firms in the market, the production of each firm is so small (dq) that does not substantially affect the price (dp).

However, all of the above don't actually mean that the individual demand curve for the firm is a horizontal line. For **after** reaching equilibrium, the price in the market is one and the same, even in oligopoly and even in duopoly, without this implying that the individual demand curve for the firm became a horizontal line. Because, **after** the moment that the stable equilibrium price prevailed in the market with the numerous firms of perfect competition  and this price becomes known to both sides of the market (consumers and producers), it is apparent that the consumers will demand (and find) the product at this price, while the producers will illusively consider their individual demand curve a horizontal line, since they don't need to reduce this price to increase their sales and if they set a higher price they would sell nothing.

Yet, that this means a horizontal demand curve for the firm is totally misleading and based on misinterpreted arguments, for it does not refer to the real demand forces, that is the consumers' preferences, but to a superficial, ostensible and illusive quasi-demand state which is the result of the market equilibrium (that is the single price resulted from the equilibrium established for all the transactions **after** equilibrium) and not the root cause of this equilibrium. Because demand, at both the aggregate and firm level, is something that exists **before** the market equilibrium and is formed by the consumers' preferences, which remain unchanged after equilibrium (for an extensive analysis and justification see Appendix A).

• There is another major inconsistency in the neoclassical theory of perfect competition that must  be noted (see <u>Figure 2</u>):

If we start examining the long-term equilibrium at firm level via the typical firm with the optimal size that is in equilibrium producing at the minimum long-term average cost, which also defines the long-term equilibrium price (p) according to the Neoclassicals, and then we move to the market level, the total supply and demand curves of the market must intersect at that price level (point A). However, that price cannot satisfy the aggregate profit maximization, because this profit maximization is achieved at the intersection of the aggregate marginal revenue curve (MR) with the total supply curve (point B); but this intersection lies necessarily, as illustrated in the graph, to the left of the intersection of the total demand and supply curves and consequently it will always provide an equilibrium price (P) higher (point E) than the equilibrium price at firm level (p).

• The fundamental principle of the neoclassical theory that the equilibrium price is determined at the intersection of total supply and total demand at market level -that is at macroeconomic level- is in contradiction to the equally basic principle of the same theory that the price of long-term equilibrium is determined at the lowest cost of the long-term average cost (LAC) curve -that is at microeconomic level. Because, while according to the latter principle the equilibrium price is fixed, according to the first principle it depends on the total demand and the total supply that arise in the market.

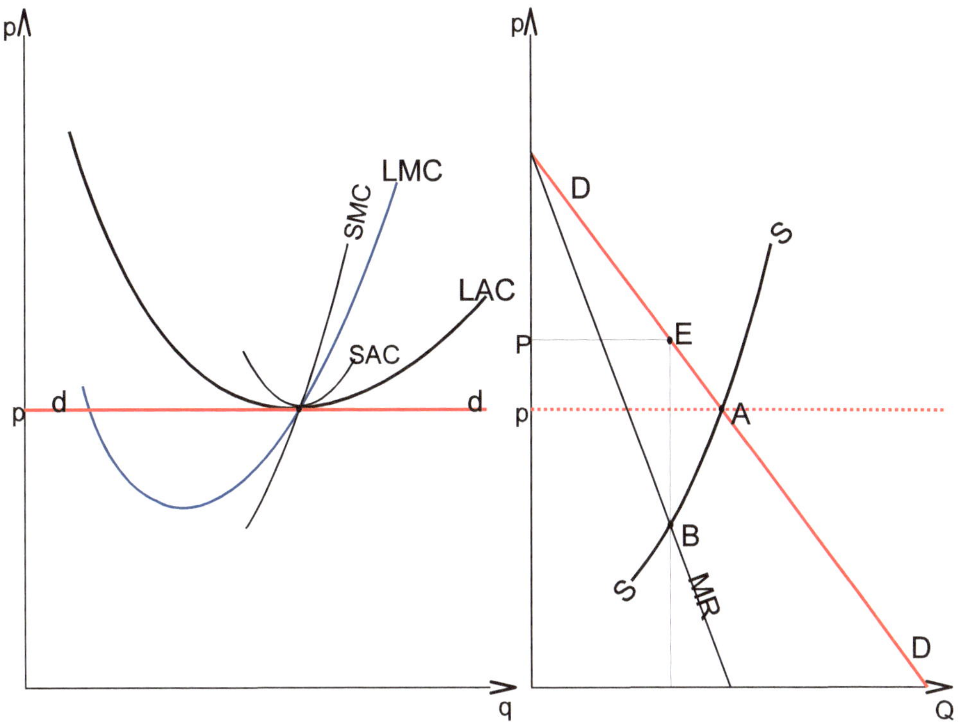


**FIGURE 2**

**The Inconsistency of the Conventional Theory**

The intersection of the market's total supply and total demand curves cannot maximize the aggregate profit of the industry.

## 3.  The Real Individual Demand Curves for the Firms

All the above beg the apparent question: how are the real individual demand curves for the firms like?

Cournot's (1838) thesis on this question was connected with his infamous concept of "best response" for every firm, which involved individual demand curves with the same slope as the total demand curve of the market and resulted in a final stable equilibrium with the aggregate demand quantity equally shared among the producers (see <u>Figure 3</u>), assuming of course equal production costs. It is worth mentioning that this was valid for a market with any number of competitive firms, from monopoly to perfect competition. This final result for final equilibrium with the total demand equally shared among the producers seems absolutely rational, but the individual demand curve for each firm seems strange to be same as the total demand shifted to the left (analogically to the number of firms), simply because the sum of all of those individual demand curves doesn't give the total demand for each price, but only for the equilibrium price. This paradox comes from the odd (and erroneous) Cournot's perception that the choice of a producer to produce a specific quantity reduced the residual demand for the rest of the producers by this constant quantity for every price of the product; that is, the residual demand for the rest of the producers was cut down for every price by the quantity that the first producer decided to produce. Of course, after the successive counteractions between the producers (the infamous Cournot's concept of "best response"), the eventually resulting equilibrium involved equally shared quantities among them -which is absolutely reasonable for a uniform producers' cost- but, due to the  erroneous perception about the individual demand curves, the point of final equilibrium, i.e. the final equilibrium price and quantity was wrong (see more in Appendix A). So, the "best response concept" of Cournot is wrong and the same stands also for the subsequent Nash game theory which is based on that Cournot concept.

The mistake can be very simply corrected if  from the outset we take the right individual demand curve for the firms. And this is no other than the total demand equally distributed among the firms. This is completely sensible, since for every price total demand is equally shared among firms due to product homogeneity and hence indifference of the consumers as to the choice of the selling firm, and can be considered a self-evident axiom.

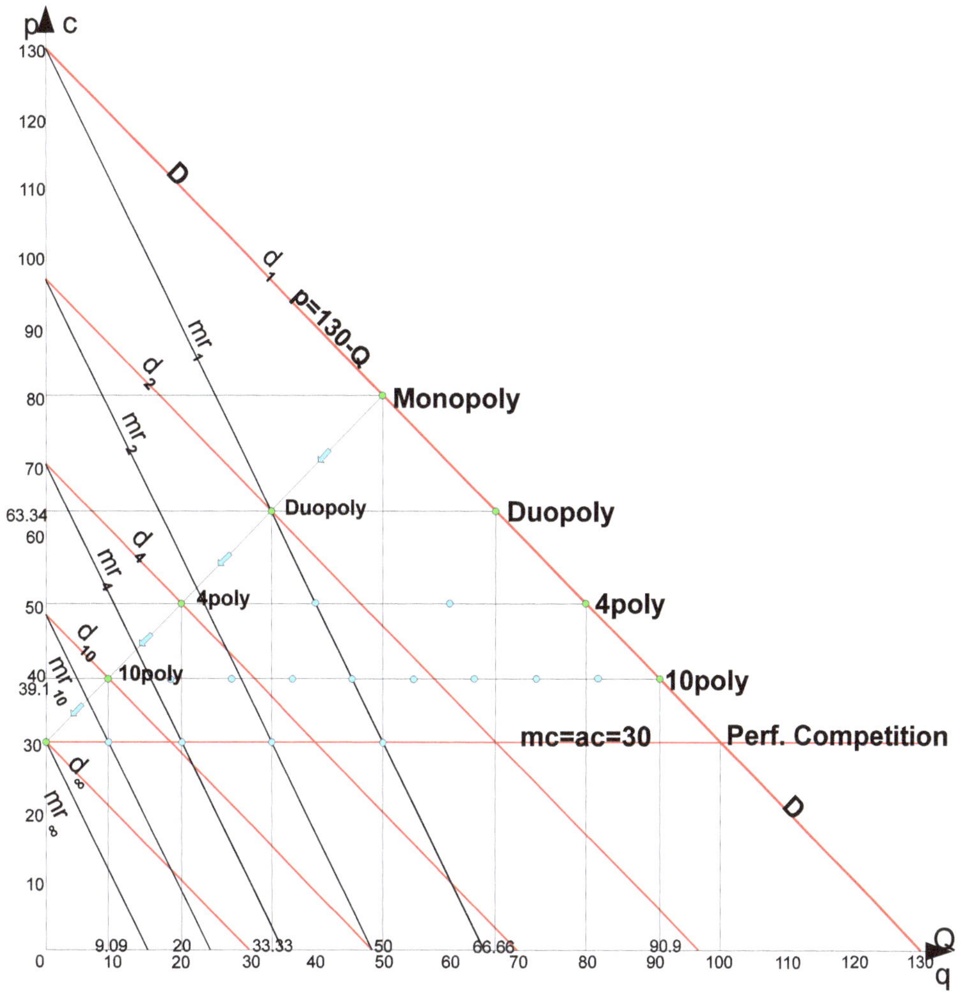



**FIGURE 3**

**Cournot Equilibrium with various numbers of firms in the market**

The Individual Demand Curves for the firms are in every case sloped.

The Equilibrium of Firm is determined by the intersection of its marginal revenue with marginal cost (=30, here). In Equilibrium, the Total Demand is equally distributed among the firms according to their number.

In Perfect Competition, price tends to marginal cost and the equilibrium point tends to the intersection of the individual demand curve-marginal revenue-marginal cost, which lies on the price-axis.

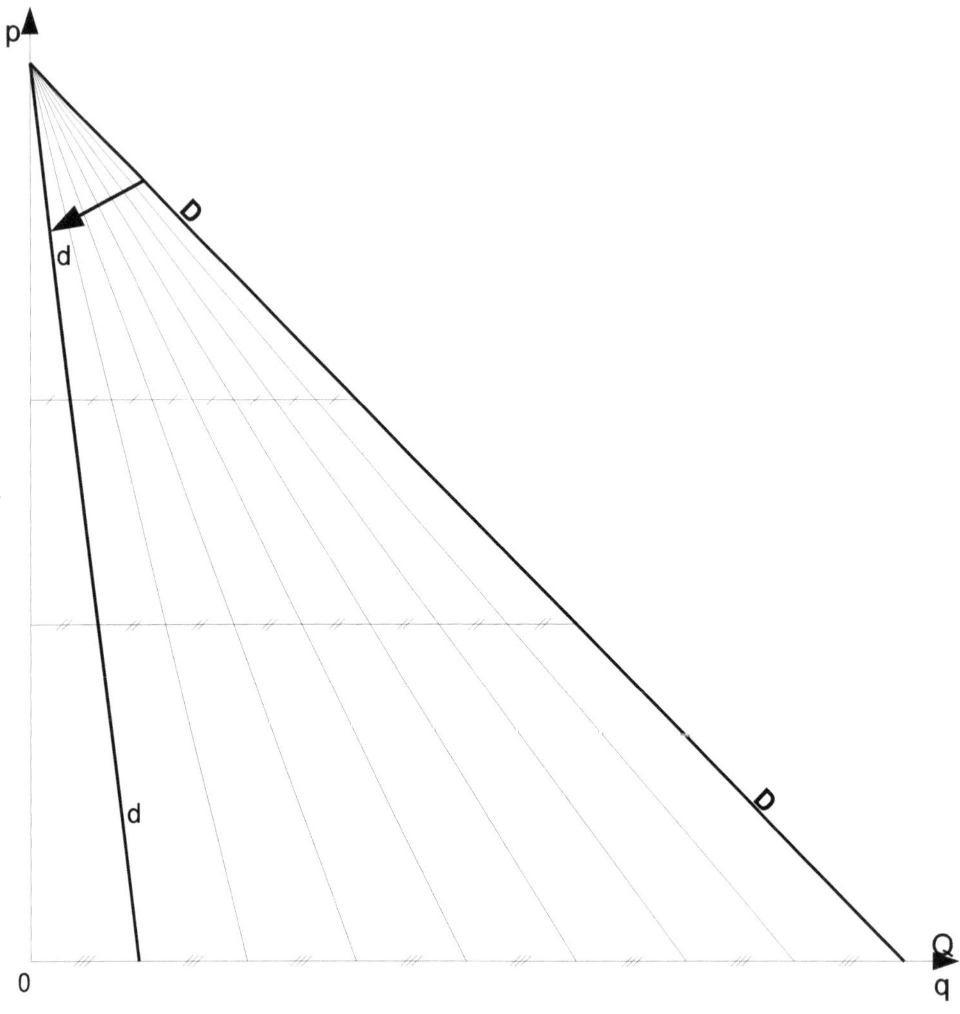



**FIGURE 4**

**The Real Individual Demand Curves for the Firms (for a market with eight firms)**

They distribute evenly the total demand among the firms at any price
and they sum up to the total demand.

This self-evident principle leads to individual demand curves for the firms that equally distribute the total demand among the firms at any price of the product[3] (see Figure 4). This implies that to find the individual demand curve for the typical firm (dd), we rotate the total demand curve downwards around its peak on price-axis analogically to the number of firms.

So, to maximize the firm's profit, the equilibrium for every firm takes place at the intersection between the marginal revenue that comes from such sloping (and not horizontal) individual demand curve and the marginal cost of the firm. Figure 5 shows the equilibrium in a market with 1, 2, 4 and 10 firms. For reasons of comparison of the results against those of the Cournot example showed in Fig. 3, the total demand and the cost are kept unchanged. We remark that, in contrast with Cournot theory, price remains the same regardless of the number of firms (provided the marginal cost is constant). We also observe that the aggregate profit of industry (rectangular area between constant price and marginal cost) remains stable regardless of the number of firms, equals the profit that would be obtained by a monopolistic exploitation of the market, and is equally distributed among the (like) firms. This find constitutes a new integrated consideration of market equilibrium, that applies to a market with any number of firms, that is from monopoly, duopoly and oligopoly to perfect competition (see next).

---

[3] In my previous paper (Nomidis 2015a), the individual demand curve is presented parallel to the total demand, but that was due to the fact that the two curves were not presented together in the same chart, but in two adjacent charts, and the scale of the total demand's quantity-axis was multiplied by the number of firms (compared to the individual demand scale). This resulted in the two curves looking parallel, while actually the individual demand curve has a slope multiplied by the number of firms compared to that of total demand, as it can be observed in the present Figure 4. The two graphs were also depicted in this way for educative reasons.

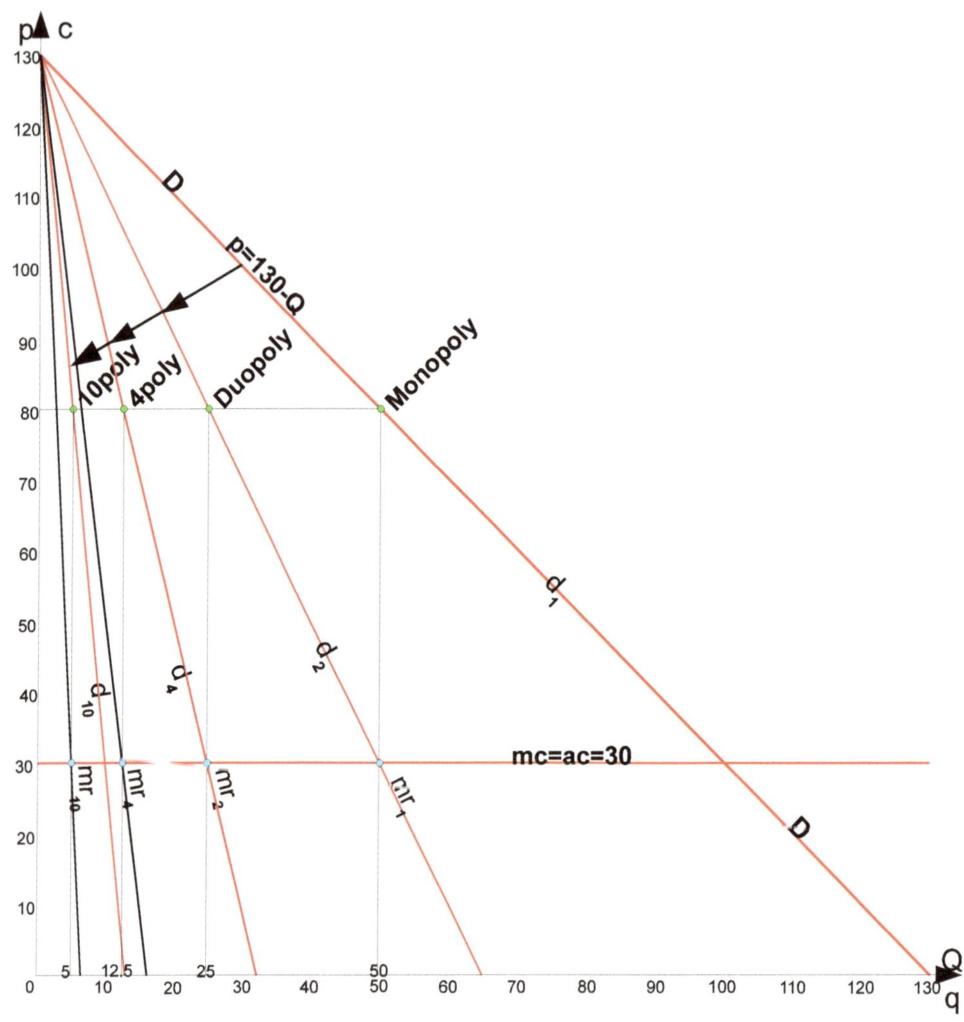


## FIGURE 5

**Equilibrium with various numbers of firms in the market, according to the New Approach**

In contrast with the Cournot theory, price remains stable regardless of the number of firms (provided that the marginal cost is constant). The aggregate profit of the industry remains stable regardless of the number of firms, equals the profit that would be achieved by a monopolistic exploitation of the market and is equally distributed among the like firms.

# 4. Perfect Competition

## *4.1. The Profit and its Monopolistic Character*

For a more analytical study of the profit under the new consideration, a numerical example is cited below with a 10-firms market, with a more developed cost form, graphically presented in <u>Figure 6</u>. We are always examining, according to the above mentioned, a market that comprises firms of uniform size, technology and cost, which equally share the total demand, that is we are examining a market with typical firms.

Let the total demand curve be given by the linear function:
$$p=130-0.5Q=130-0.5nq$$
The marginal revenue from the total demand is therefore:
$$MR=130-Q=130-nq$$
If the industry for this market involves 10 firms, the individual demand for every firm is:
$$p=130-5q$$
and the marginal revenue for every firm is:
$$mr=130-10q$$

Let now the total cost of the typical firm be given by the function:
$$tc=1.5q^2+f=1.5q^2+400$$
where f is the fixed cost (=400) and $1.5q^2$ the variable cost (mainly wages and raw materials).
The marginal cost of the firm will then be:
$$mc=3q$$
and the profit function for every firm will be:
$$\pi = p\cdot q\text{-}tc = p\cdot q\text{-}(1.5q^2+f)$$

The profit maximization of the firm takes place at the intersection of its marginal revenue with its marginal cost (since $d\pi/dq = mr\text{-}mc = 0$):
$$mr=mc \quad or \quad 130-10q=3q$$
From the above condition, the equilibrium point for the firm results:
$$\mathbf{q=10} \quad \text{and hence} \quad \mathbf{p=130-5q=80}$$
and the maximized profit of the firm:
$$\pi = p\cdot q\text{-}1.5q^2\text{-}f = 80\cdot10-1.5\cdot10^2-400 = 250$$
$$\mathbf{\pi = 250}$$

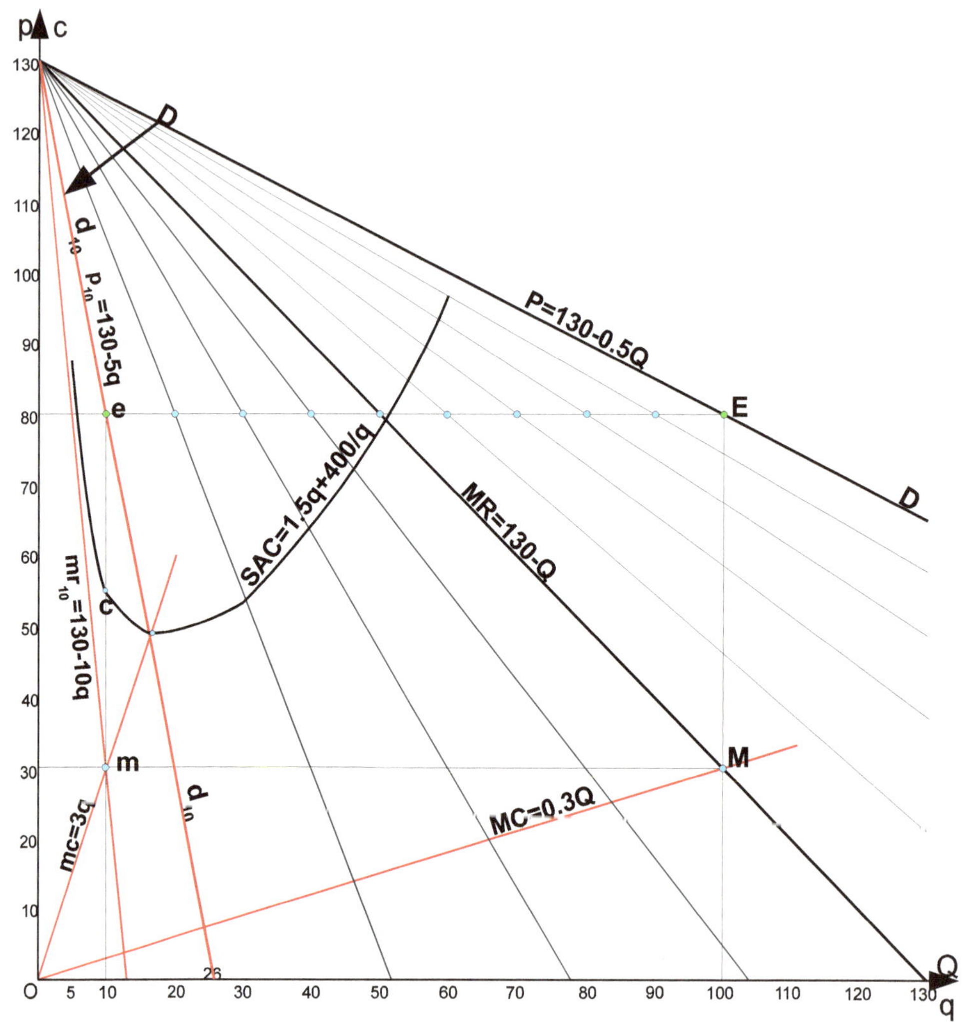



**FIGURE 6**

**Equilibrium in a market with 10 firms**

The equilibrium price for the firm equals that of a monopoly with the same cost as the aggregated cost of the firms, regardless of the number of firms. The aggregate profit (before fixed cost) of the industry equals the profit that would be achieved by a monopolistic exploitation of the market (OME80O) and is equally distributed among the like firms (Ome80O). The profit per product unit **ce** decreases with the entrance of new firms (rotation of individual demand curve dd to the left) until in perfect competition becomes zero (tangency of dd with the SAC curve).

If we examine the aggregate profit of all the firms of the industry, we will find that this is: $\Pi = 10 \cdot 250 = \mathbf{2500}$

It is easy to prove that this aggregate profit results also from the aggregate values of the market, that is from the intersection of the aggregate marginal revenue coming from the total market demand with the aggregate marginal cost of the firms, which, as known, represents the total supply curve of the market:

MR=MC     or     130-Q=3Q/10=0.3Q     (since MC=mc=3q=3Q/10)

where MC is the horizontal sum of the mc curves (just as MR is the horizontal sum of mr) and for this reason it has the same value as mc (sum of the quantities under the same value).

From the above condition, the equilibrium point for the overall market results:

$$\mathbf{Q=100} \ (=10 \times 10) \qquad \mathbf{p}=130-0.5 \cdot 100=\mathbf{80}$$

The aggregate cost of the industry (since its marginal cost is MC=0.3Q) is:

$$TC=0.15Q^2+F=0.15Q^2+10f$$

or otherwise:     $TC=10tc=10(1.5q^2+f)=15q^2+10f=0.15Q^2+10f$

and the maximized aggregate profit of all the firms of the industry:

$$\Pi = pQ\text{-}TC = pQ\text{-}0.15Q^2\text{-}10f = 80 \cdot 100 - 0.15 \cdot 100^2 - 10 \cdot 400 = \mathbf{2500}$$

i.e. the same as the previously calculated one firm's profit multiplied by the 10 firms of the industry.[4]

This means that the overall profit of the industry would be the same if the industry consisted of just one monopolistic firm -which thus would reap the benefit of the total demand of the market- and the cost of this monopoly was the sum of costs of the individual firms (which is interpreted as a monopoly consisted of all the firms of the industry being running separately); and this would be valid for any number of firms in the industry. This means that the overall profit of the industry, which would come from a monopolistic exploitation of the market, is evenly distributed among the firms of the industry. In other words, the overall industry profit is equal to the profit that would result from a monopolistic exploitation of the market and is evenly distributed among the firms, whichever the number of firms in that industry is. This outcome highlights that both the aggregate market of a product and the firms that it comprises operate as

---

[4] Note that the profit (before fixed cost) is represented by the area OME80O for the industry (aggregate) and Ome80O for the single firm, since the areas below the marginal cost curves MC and mc indicate the relevant variable cost.

monopolies, and this is due to the fact that the demand curve of both the market and the firms (among which the market demand is distributed) have negative slope and are not horizontal lines.

In Fgure 6, the profit per product unit appears as the distance **ce** between the average cost curve (SAC) and the individual demand curve for the firm (d10, when the number of firms is 10). This profit attracts new firms to enter the market and so is gradually decreasing as the number of firms increases. This becomes apparent in the graph since by the entry of new firms and the increase of their number, the individual demand curve for the firm rotates to the left, which decreases the distance **ce** i.e. the profit of the firm. This process continues until in perfect competition the individual demand curve for the firm becomes tangent to the averge cost curve (SAC) and thus the profit becomes zero since then *price=average cost* (see next Section).

### 4.2. *Perfect Competition, but still with Monopolistic Character*

The previous rule of the overall industry profit equally distributed among the firms of the industry in combination with the zero profit in perfect competition determines the number of firms that constitute an industry having reached the state of perfect competition:

Since the overall profit of the industry (equal to the profit that would come from a monopolistic exploitation of the market) is equally distributed among the firms of the industry, the profit of each firm will decrease as the number of firms increases; on the other hand, the number of firms will increase until their economic profit (i.e. the profit over the normal one) becomes zero in perfect competition (i.e. until their profit equals the normal profit yielded in every other business activity). So, one can determine the number of firms in perfect competition, which, based on the previous rule of equally shared aggregate profit, gives for each firm a zero economic profit, or otherwise an economic profit, before deducting the fixed cost, that just covers the fixed cost of the firm (including the normal profit). For this purpose, an example similar to the previous one is given below (see also Figure 7).

Let the total demand curve be given by the linear function:    $p=130-0.5Q$
The marginal revenue from the total demand is therefore:        $MR=130-Q$

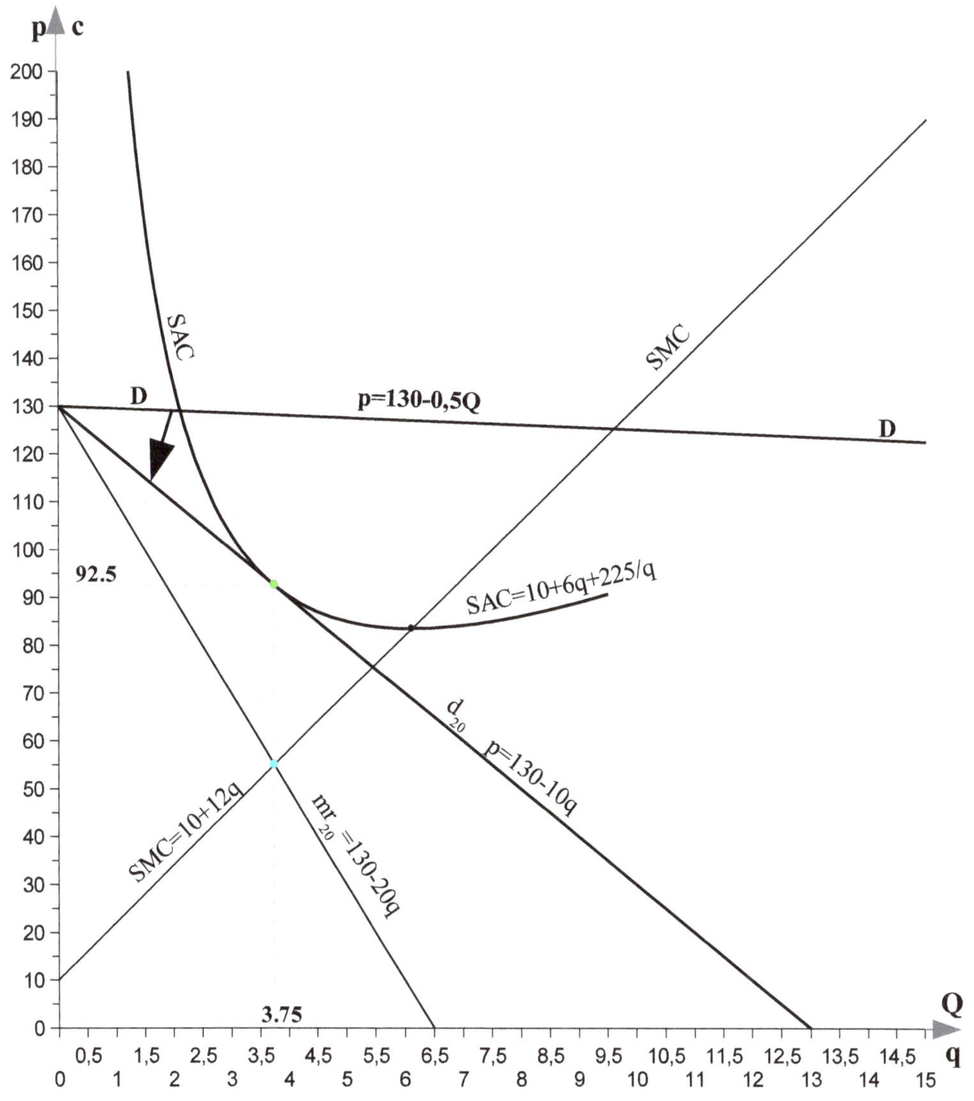



**FIGURE 7. Short-Term Perfect Competition**

Schematically, the individual demand curve and the equilibrium point for the firm in perfect competition are determined by the rotation of the total demand curve around its peak on the price-axis downwards until it becomes tangential to the short-term average cost curve (SAC) of the firm.

The resultant equilibrium point lies vertically above the intersection of marginal revenue (mr) with marginal cost (SMC) (profit maximization condition) and the equilibrium price equals the average cost (zero economic profit due to perfect competition). The sharing of the industry's revenue among the firms just covers their fixed and variable cost.

No need for a vast number of firms for perfect competition (just 20 in this example).

If the perfectly competitive industry for this market involves **"n" firms**, the individual demand for every firm is: $\qquad$ p=130-0.5·n·q

and the marginal revenue for every firm is: $\qquad$ mr=130-n·q

Let now the total cost of the typical firm be: $\qquad$ tc=10q+6q²+f

where f is the fixed cost and $10q+6q^2$ the variable cost (mainly wages and raw materials).

The marginal cost of the firm will then be: $\qquad$ mc=10+12q

and the profit function for every firm will be: $\qquad$ $\pi = p·q - (10q+6q^2+f)$

Assuming a fixed cost of, let say, f=225 (including normal profit), the economic profit becomes zero when:

(1) $\qquad$ $\pi = p·q-(10q+ 6q^2+f) = (130-0.5nq)q-(10q+6q^2+225)=0$

The profit maximizing condition on the other hand (even if this profit=zero) is:

(2) $\qquad$ mr=mc $\qquad$ or $\qquad$ 130-nq=10+12q

The solution of the previous system of two equations gives (see also Figure 7):

$\qquad$ **q=3.75** $\qquad$ **n=20** $\qquad$ and consequently $\qquad$ **p=130-0.5nq=92.5**

It is easy to prove that the aggregate profit of the perfectly competitive industry equally distributed among the firms gives for each firm a profit, before deducting the fixed cost, that just covers the fixed cost of the firm (including the normal profit):

The total production of the perfectly competitive industry, which in this example consists of 20 firms, is: $\qquad$ **Q=n·q=20·3.75=75**

and again the equilibrium price of the market: $\qquad$ **p=130-0.5Q=92.5**

The aggregate profit of the perfectly competitive industry, before deducting fixed costs, is:

$\Pi=pQ-20(10q+6q^2)=pQ-20(10Q/20+6Q^2/20^2)=92,5·75-10·75-6·75^2/20=4500$

This aggregate profit before deducting fixed costs is evenly distributed among the 20 competitive firms of the industry, each firm getting:

$\qquad$ $\pi= 4500/20=225$

an amount just covering the firm's fixed cost f=225 (including normal profit).

All of the above raise the question whether it really needs to be a vast number of firms for the existence of perfect competition, as argued by the neoclassical theory; and whether the equilibrium price is stable because of the vast number of firms and the consequent so infinitesimal individual production that a potential variation in it doesn't affect the equilibrium price. As it becomes apparent from the previous example, neither the former nor the latter need happen. The number of firms that constitute the perfectly competitive industry with zero profit due to competition is just 20, and an increase in total production due to entrance of a new firm would considerably bring down the equilibrium price from 92.5 to 91.78, as this is derived from the profit maximization condition for the 21 firms:

$$mr=mc \; \rightarrow \; 130\text{-}21{\cdot}q=10+12q \; \rightarrow \; q=3.64 \; \rightarrow \; Q=21{\cdot}3.64=76.44 \; \rightarrow$$
$$p=130\text{-}0.5{\cdot}76.44=91.78$$

The fact that the equilibrium price remains stable at the 92.5 level is not due to the individual demand curve being a horizontal line at this level, neither due to the number of firms being so large, and consequently the individual production so small, that a variation in it would not considerably impact the equilibrium price. The real reason is that this equilibrium price yields the normal profit for every of the 20 firms, while any movement of the individual production away from this equilibrium production (increase or decrease) or the entrance of a new firm into the market would cause an economic loss to every firm, because this would bring the price below the average cost (SAC=10+6q+225/q), since the individual demand curve osculates the average cost curve at that equilibrium point, see Figure 7; and for this reason this is not actualized; on the other hand, the exit of a firm from the market would cause a profit over the normal one and therefore the entrance of a new firm and the restoration of the equilibrium back to its previous state with a zero economic profit.

Therefore the prerequisite of the vast number of firms set by the neoclassical theory of perfect competition is not valid and has to be retired along with the horizontal individual demand curve concept. The emphasis in the definition of perfect competition should be placed on the economic profit being zero and the entry-exit of firms until this is realized.

Schematically, the equilibrium process, connected to the gradually increasing number of firms due to extra profit, is represented by the rotation of the total demand curve around its peak on the price-axis downwards until, in perfect competition, it becomes tangential to the short-term average cost curve (SAC) of the firm and then the profit becomes zero as then *price=average cost*. This point of tangency is the resultant equilibrium point and at the same time corresponds vertically to the intersection of the marginal revenue (mr) with the short-term marginal cost (SMC), thus accomplishing also the profit maximization condition. The sharing of the industry's revenue among the firms just covers their fixed and variable cost (zero economic profit) and there is no need for a vast number of firms for perfect competition (just 20 in this example).

To complete the view on the individual firm and its equilibrium in perfect competition, one has to obtain, in the previous numerical example, the average cost curve for the firm and check whether the individual demand curve osculates this curve at the equilibrium point derived from the previous numerical example for perfect competition (see also Appendices B and C.2 of this paper). Indeed, the average cost curve for the firm (precisely speaking, the short-term average cost SAC) is (see also Figure 7):

$$c = C/q = (10q+6q^2+f)/q = 10+6q+225/q$$

and for the equilibrium quantity q=3.75 derived previously for perfect competition, this function gives:

$$c = 10+6 \cdot 3.75+225/3.75 = 92.5$$

that is, average cost equal to the derived equilibrium price in perfect competition. The tangent of this function at the above point of the curve (which coincides with the equilibrium point) is:

$$dc/dq = 6-225/q^2 = 6-225/3.75^2 = -10$$

that is, it has the slope of the individual demand curve of the firm (p=130-10q).

In addition, it is easily verified the well-known property that the average cost curve (SAC) has a minimum at its intersection with the marginal cost curve (SMC, see Fig.7).

### 4.3. Long-Term Perfect Competition

If the perfect competition is examined under the long-term view, then we must consider that the production factors' quantities have the possibility to vary over time (this is especially true for capital, as labor is already a variable even in the short run). In this case, no part of the cost is fixed, that is all cost parts are variable attributed to the varied production factors. The numerical example that follows provides clarity on the above and is depicted in Figure 8.

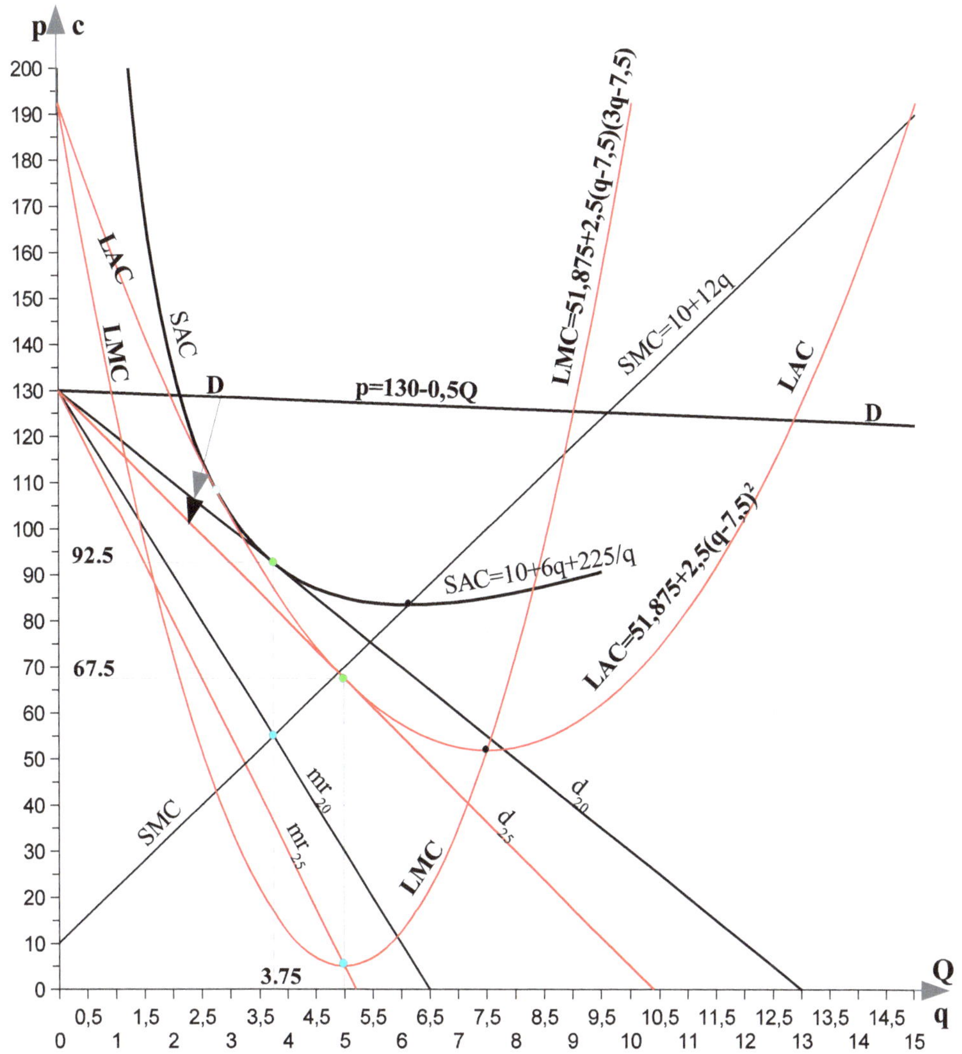


## FIGURE 8

### Long-Term Perfect Competition

Schematically, the individual demand curve and the equilibrium point for the firm in perfect competition are determined by the rotation of the total demand curve around its peak on the price-axis downwards until it becomes tangential to the long-term average cost curve (LAC) of the firm.

The resultant equilibrium point lies vertically above the intersection of marginal revenue (mr) with marginal cost (LMC) (profit maximization condition) and the equilibrium price equals the average cost (zero economic profit due to perfect competition). The sharing of the industry's revenue among the firms just covers all their variable (due to the long term) costs (zero economic profit).

No need for a vast number of firms for perfect competition (just 25 in this example).

The total demand curve is kept the same: $\qquad$ p = 130-0.5Q

so the individual demand for every firm is: $\qquad$ p = 130-0.5·n·q

where **"n"** the number of firms

and the marginal revenue for every firm is: $\qquad$ mr = 130-nq.

Let now the long-term average cost (LAC) for every firm be given by the function: $\qquad$ **LAC** = c = 51.875+2.5(q-7.5)$^2$

so its total cost is: $\qquad$ tc = 51.875q+2.5q (q-7.5)$^2$ $\qquad$ (all cost parts variable)

and its marginal cost is:

$$\textbf{LMC}=mc=51.875+2.5[(q-7.5)^2+2q\,(q-7.5)]=51.875+2.5(q-7.5)(3q-7.5)$$

The economic profit of each firm becomes zero (due to perfect competition) when

(1) $\qquad$ $\pi = p\cdot q - c\cdot q = 0 \;\rightarrow\; p{=}c \;\rightarrow\; 130\text{-}0.5nq{=}51.875{+}2.5(q{-}7.5)^2$

The profit maximizing condition on the other hand (even if this profit=zero) is:

(2) $\qquad$ mr=mc $\rightarrow$ $\;$ 130-nq=51.875+2.5(q-7.5)(3q-7.5)

The solution of the previous system of two equations gives: $\quad$ **q=5** $\quad$ **n=25**

hence, the equilibrium price of perfect competition derives: $\quad$ **p**=130-0.5nq=**67.5**

and the total production of the perfectly competitive industry, which consists of 25 firms, is: $\qquad$ Q=n·q=125

Schematically, the equilibrium process, connected to the gradually increasing number of firms due to extra profit, is represented by the rotation of the total demand curve around its peak on the price-axis downwards until, in perfect competition, it becomes tangential to the long-term average cost curve (LAC) of the firm and then the profit becomes zero as then *price=average cost*. This point of tangency is the resultant equilibrium point and at the same time corresponds vertically to the intersection of the marginal revenue (mr) with the long-term marginal cost (LMC), thus accomplishing also the profit maximization condition. The sharing of the industry's revenue among the firms just covers their variable (due to the long term) costs (zero economic profit) and there is no need for a vast number of firms for perfect competition (just 25 in this example).

## 5. The Invalidation of the Neoclassical Theory and its Implications

The sloping individual demand curve for the firm brings about a total invalidation of the conventional Perfect Competition and Social Welfare theories and a radical reformation of the whole Value economic theory. The key implications that this reformation brings to the economic theory are briefly presented below.

### *5.1. Equilibrium Price and Cost – Non-Maximization of the Social Welfare*

According to the neoclassic theory of perfect competition, the long-term equilibrium point of the firm lies at the lowest point of the long-term average cost curve LAC. This happens because of the supposedly horizontal line of the individual demand of the firm, which at that point becomes tangential to the LAC curve (see Figure 9) thus resulting in zero economic profit due to perfect competition and consequently in the equalization of price to the average cost. The short-term cost curves of the enterprise, SAC for the average cost and SMC for the marginal cost, that correspond to this optimal size of production also pass from this long-term equilibrium point. The above conditions have as result the size of this enterprise to be considered the socially "optimal size" since it implies the lowest possible average cost, and hence price as well, while the respective production level to be the socially "ideal output" (Harrod 1934, Kahn 1935), which implies null "excess capacity" (Cassels 1936, Ferguson 1956). Most importantly, price (representing as known the marginal social benefit) equals in this case marginal cost as well (reflecting generally also the social marginal cost[5]), condition that leads to the maximization of the social welfare (maximum consumer-producer result). This result becomes apparent at the market level (right side in Figure 9), where social welfare, i.e. the sum of consumer and producer surpluses, is maximized at the intersection **A** of the total demand and supply curves (social welfare is then represented by the area DASD).

However under the new revised theory, these results are not true. Due to the negative slope of the individual demand curve of the firm, its osculation point **e** with the LAC curve (which constitutes the long-term equilibrium point with again zero economic profit due to competition) lies to the left of the minimum average

---

[5] Except for the case of external economies (positive or negative ones).

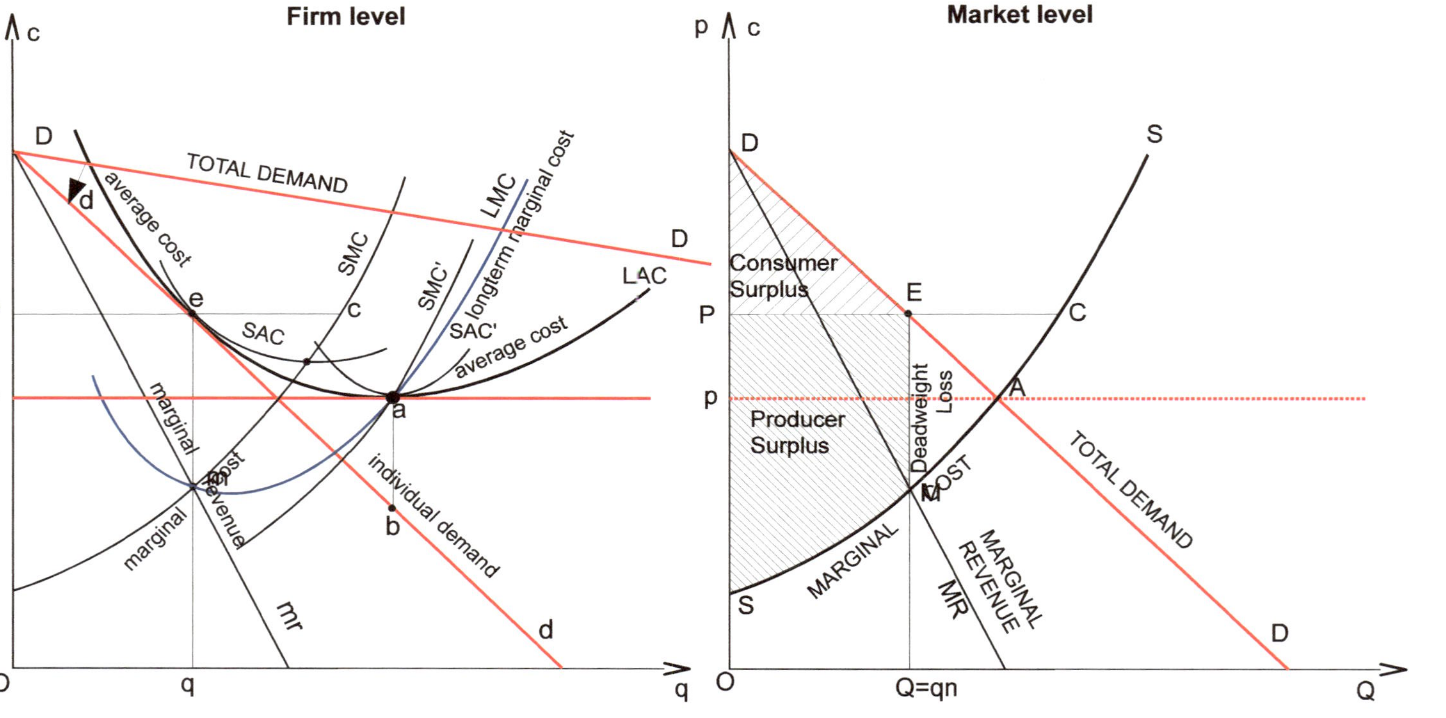


**FIGURE 9.  The Social Welfare's Deterioration**

The new consideration implies equilibrium with a price (P) higher than the ideal price of the minimum possible average cost (p) and also higher than the marginal cost (qm=QM), size of enterprise (SAC) smaller than the optimum size (SAC$_o$), and production level per firm (q) smaller than the ideal output (q$_o$), with a negative excess capacity.

These effects move the social welfare away from its maximum level. Social welfare (sum of consumer and producer surpluses) declines from its maximum value DASD (according to the neoclassical theory) to DEMSD (according to the new reformed theory) creating a deadweight loss AEM.

cost **a** at higher cost levels (see Figure 9). The implication of the above is that the enterprise operates with a smaller size than the optimum (SAC instead of $SAC_o$), which implies an average cost -and hence price- higher than the minimum average cost of production, and a production level (and consequently employment) lower than the "ideal output", which in turn implies negative "excess capacity". What is worse, price does not equal marginal cost, which does not lead to maximization of the social welfare, while the previous deviations from the ideal norms makeeven worse the decline of the social welfare from its maximum. This again becomes apparent at the market level, where social welfare is then represented by the area DEBSD, which is less than the maximum value DASD, leaving a social deadweight loss represented by the area EABE.

## 5.2. *Invalidation of the Marginal Productivity theory of Income Distribution*

In addition, the moving of the equilibrium away from the minimum point of the average cost curve invalidates the marginal productivity theory of income distribution, according to which labor and the other production factors are remunerated by the value of their marginal product, because the whole of the above theory applies only if the equilibrium takes place at the minimum of the average cost curve **a** (where constant returns to scale occur).

## 5.3. *Monopolistic Character of Perfect Competition and Integration of Market Theory*

Since the individual demand curves for the firms are not horizontal (as the neoclassical theory states) but sloped, like the total demand, the business behavior of the firms and their profit have a monopolistic character and the same is valid for the whole industry of the market. The aggregate profit of the industry (which is maximized, as opposed to that in the neoclassical theory) equals the profit that would come from a monopolistic use of the market and is evenly distributed among the individual firms of the industry, whichever their number is (provided they all have same costs) (see Figures 5 and 6).

This result provides the basis for a single integrated theory of market equilibrium for any number of firms, that is from a monopoly, duopoly, oligopoly, to perfect competition. It also provides the basis for the determination of the number of firms with zero economic profit under perfect competition.

## 5.4. Implications on the Labor Market

The sloping individual demand curve for the firm results in a labor demand curve of the firm not being represented by the value of marginal product (VMP) of the labor (as the neoclassical theory states) but by the marginal revenue product (MRP), which implies a monopolistic exploitation of the labor and lower levels of wages and employment[6]. On the other hand, from the employees' side this time, the exploitation of their monopolistic power on labor -by means of labor unions- for the maximization of their aggregate share they can reap from the demand for their labor, leads to even lower employment levels and deterioration of the unemployment effect.

In conclusion, the labor market leads inevitably to a move of the social welfare away from its optimum state. This is an unavoidable aftereffect of the monopolistic exploitation that both firms and employees apply on the good they provide to the market, namely the product for the firms and the labor for the employees, in order to maximize their benefit.[6]

## 5.5. Maximization of the Industry Profit from the Aggregate Demand

Under the new revised theory, the market equilibrium is not determined anymore by the infamous principle of the intersection of the total supply and total demand curves, but by the intersection of the total supply (specifically, the aggregated individual marginal costs) with the aggregate marginal revenue that comes from the total demand. In this way the integrated profit of all the industry's production as a whole is maximized (since each firm maximizes its profit), while the neoclassical intersection of total supply and total demand does not accomplish this condition for profit maximization which the Neoclassicals themselves have set as presupposition; or, to put it in other words, the neoclassical equilibrium does not fully exploit the total demand of the market from the side of the firms and therefore it cannot be the equilibrium point of the market.

---

[6] For a comprehensive analysis see Nomidis (2015b).

### 5.6. *The Long-term Equilibrium Price depends not only on Cost but also on Demand*

The price of the long-term equilibrium, according to the neoclassical theory of perfect competition, is also determined by the lowest level of the long-term average cost (LAC), independently of the position and shape of the total demand curve in the market. According to the new revised theory, however, the price of the long-term equilibrium depends crucially on the position and shape of the demand curve (see <u>Figure 9</u>), beyond of course its dependence on the position and shape of the LAC curve. Especially, it depends strongly on the peak point of the demand curve on the price-axis. The higher this demand peak point is, the higher the equilibrium price will be compared to the ideal price of the minimum average cost, and the smaller the production level will be compared to the "ideal output" and the size of the enterprise compared to the "optimal size".

The only case for the equilibrium price to take the ideal value of the lowest average cost would occur if the demand curve became horizontal. This case is certainly a very rare case and if this happened, it would apply both at firm and at market level. Nevertheless this could be possible if all the consumers demanded the product at (or, in other words, offered for the product) only one and the same price independently of the demanded quantity. Then, this horizontal demand curve of same price would gradually take the position of the tangent to the average cost curve at its minimum level, with no profit due to competition (while in the interim stages towards equilibrium, when the number of firms has not yet reached its final value, there would be a profit gradually declining). This price position at the lowest cost level could probably happen from the beginning (without interim stages), in a free economy, if the consumers knew this lowest cost and demanded the product only at an equal price.

### 5.7. *New Definition and Prerequisites for Perfect Competition*

Price in perfect competition remains stable neither due to the horizontal individual demand curve for the firms nor due to the vast number of firms and the subsequent so small individual production of each that a variation in it would not considerably impact the equilibrium price, but due to the economic loss for every firm that would emerge from any movement of the individual production away (increase or decrease) from the equilibrium production (osculation point of demand and cost) or from the entry of a new firm into the market, because then price would become lower than average cost (see <u>Figure 7</u>); while the exit of a firm from the market would bring about an economic profit and therefore the entrance of a new firm and the restoration of the equilibrium back to its previous state with a zero economic profit.

Therefore, the prerequisite of the vast number of firms set by the neoclassical theory of perfect competition is not valid and has to be retired along with the horizontal individual demand curve concept. The emphasis in the definition of perfect competition must be placed on the economic profit being zero and the entry-exit of firms until this is realized.

## 5.8. *Macroeconomic General Equilibrium*

The new revised perfect competition theory has a considerable impact on the macroeconomic theory of General Equilibrium, where now the equation of total supply and total demand in each market has to be replaced by the equation of the total supply (which is the aggregated marginal cost of all the firms) with the aggregate marginal revenue derived from the total demand, a condition that ensures the maximization of the industry profit even if this is zero due to the perfect competition. All of the above mentioned functions (curves) are already well known and used in the General Equilibrium theory, except for the aggregate marginal revenue, which, however, derives easily from the well known function (curve) of the total demand. Therefore, the substitution is easy but at the same time very important and meaningful.

Consequently, if the demand and supply functions of the good "i" in the market are:

$$\text{Total demand } \mathbf{p_i = D_i(Q_i)} \qquad \text{Total supply } \mathbf{p_i = S_i(Q_i)}$$

then the equilibrium condition of each good market, instead of the familiar $D_i(Q_i) = S_i(Q_i)$, becomes:

$$\mathbf{d(p_iQ_i)/dQ_i = S_i(Q_i)} \quad \text{or} \quad \mathbf{p_i + p_i'Q_i = S_i(Q_i)} \quad \text{or} \quad \mathbf{D_i(Q_i) + D_i'(Q_i)Q_i = S_i(Q_i)}$$

# 6. Summary

The basic points of the new consideration are summarized below.

**1)** The individual demand curve for the firm is not perfectly elastic (horizontal), as the neoclassical theory of perfect competition claims, but has the usual form of a demand curve with negative slope.

The real demand curves for the firms distribute evenly the total demand among the competitors at any product price and they sum up to the total demand (something that should be true in the conventional economic theory, but it is not). The uniform distribution of demand among the firms is obviously due to the homogeneity of their product and the indifference of the consumers as to the choice of the seller, and it constitutes a self-evident principle (provided that, of course, there are no consumers' mobility frictions).

So, the total demand curve of the market divided by the number of firms (for each price) gives the individual demand curve for the firm. Therfore, to find the individual demand curve for the firm we rotate the total demand curve around its peak on the price-axis downwards analogically to the number of firms.

**2)** The fallacy of the theory of perfect competition about the horizontal individual demand curve for the firm has been most probably developed from a misinterpretation of a Cournot's phrase in his infamous book "Mathematical Principles of the Theory of Wealth". The original meaning of this phrase was to denote the stability of equilibrium price in perfect competition where the number of firms is very large (according to Cournot and the Neoclassicals) and thus the production of each firm is very small and unable to affect the prevalent price. This misunderstanding was probably strengthened by the fact that according to Cournot's theory the price in perfect competition tends towards the marginal cost, which is also happening when the individual demand curve for the firm is a horizontal straight line (see Appendix A).

Considering the individual demand curve horizontal is a mistake, because (besides the other reasons mentioned in this book) this is the result of the market equilibrium (i.e. the unique price resulted from the equilibrium and established for all the subsequent exchanges) and not the root cause of that equilibrium. That is, it doesn't express the real demand forces, i.e. the consumers' preferences, which of course remain the same **before** and **after** equilibrium (see Appendix A).

**3)** The long-term equilibrium of the firm takes place at the triple osculation point of the firm's individual demand curve with the long-term average cost curve (LAC) and the short-term average cost curve (SAC) of the firm. This equilibrium state corresponds also to the triple intersection of the marginal revenue, the long-term marginal cost (LMC) and the short-term marginal cost (SMC) of the firm[7], which accomplishes the maximization of the economic profit of the firm being at the same time zero due to the perfect competition.

**4) The individual equilibrium of each firm maximizing its profit automatically results also, as it is proved, in the maximization of the integrated profit of the industry that comes from the total demand of the market.**

Thus, the equilibrium at the market level is realized, by analogy to the firm level, at the intersection of the aggregate marginal cost with the total marginal revenue that comes from the total demand of the market (and not with the total demand itself, as the neoclassical theory says), which maximizes the total profit of the industry that comes from the total demand as previously said.

**5)** The previous conclusion does not hold in the neoclassical theory of perfect competition, nor could it hold (although it should), and this conclusively proves its inconsistency. The deeper reason for this is that while at market level the demand curve is sloped, at firm level it is horizontal, assumptions inconsistent with each other leading to inconsistent results. On the contrary, under the new consideration, the equilibrium of the market can be examined both at market and at firm level -by means of the individual firm demand curve- with the same consistent results.

**6)** Since the individual demand curves for the firms are not horizontal but sloped, like the total demand, the business behavior of the firms and their profit have a monopolistic character and the same is valid for the whole industry of the market. The aggregate profit of the industry (which is maximized, as opposed to

---

[7] For the proof of the above statements see Appendix C: Mathematical Validation Section C.2).

that in the neoclassical theory) equals the profit that would come from a monopolistic use of the market and is evenly distributed among the individual firms of the industry, no matter which their number is (provided they all have same costs).

**7)** This result provides the basis for a single integrated theory of market equilibrium for any number of firms; that is from a monopoly, duopoly, oligopoly, to perfect competition.

**8)** The evenly distributed among the firms maximized aggregate profit of the industry determines the number of firms in the state of perfect competition, in a way that the resulting economic profit of each firm becomes zero (this means that the share per firm just covers its fixed and variable cost (including normal profit)).

Schematically, the individual demand curve and the equilibrium point for the firm in perfect competition are determined by the rotation of the total demand curve around its peak on the price-axis downwards until it becomes tangential to the average cost curve of the firm. This tangency point is the equilibrium point.

**9)** Price in perfect competition remains stable neither due to the horizontal individual demand curve for the firms nor due to the vast number of firms and the subsequent so small individual production of each firm that a variation in it would not considerably impact the equilibrium price, but due to the economic loss for every firm that would emerge from any movement of the individual production away (increase or decrease) from the equilibrium production (osculation point of demand and cost) or from the entry of a new firm into the market, because then price would become lower than average cost; while the exit of a firm from the market would bring about an economic profit and therefore the entrance of a new firm and the restoration of the equilibrium back to its previous state with a zero economic profit.

Therefore, the prerequisite of the vast number of firms set by the neoclassical theory of perfect competition is not valid and has to be retired along with the horizontal individual demand curve concept. The emphasis must be placed upon the zero economic profit condition and the entry-exit of firms until this is realized.

**10)** The above results totally invalidate the conventional neoclassical theories of Perfect Competition and Social Welfare and dramatically reform the Theory of Value and other basic pillars of the economic theory, since:

**a.** The equilibrium price is not determined anymore by the traditional intersection of total supply with total demand, but by the intersection of total supply with the marginal revenue coming from the total demand.

**b.** The long-term equilibrium price is not equal to the minimum average cost, as stated in the neoclassical theory, but it is always higher.

**c.** Social welfare is not maximized, as claimed by the neoclassical theory, since now price is not equal to the marginal cost and also since it is higher than the minimum average cost.

**d.** Labor is not paid according  to the value of its marginal product but according to the marginal product revenue, which implies the monopolistic exploitation of labor and lower wage and employment levels and in fact worsens the previous social welfare's deterioration.

**e.** The competition of firms, even the perfect competition, has a monopolistic character due to the negative slope of the demand curve at both the market and the firm level. The aggregate profit of the industry equals the profit that would come from a monopolistic use of the market and is evenly distributed among the individual firms of the industry, whichever their number is. This result provides the basis for a single integrated theory of market equilibrium for any number of firms, that is from a monopoly to perfect competition.

**f.** The prerequisite of the vast number of firms set by the neoclassical theory of perfect competition is not valid and has to be retired along with the horizontal individual demand curve concept. The emphasis must be placed upon the zero economic profit condition and the entry-exit of firms until this is realized.

**g.** The macroeconomic theory of general equilibrium has to be revised taking into consideration the new theory of market equilibrium.

# 7. Conclusion

The correction of the wrong concept of price taking and horizontal demand curve for the firm and the adoption of the appropriate sloped individual demand curve entails the monopolistic character of the market even under perfect competition and a total and dramatic reformation of the neoclassical theory of Perfect Competition, Value, Social Welfare and other major fields of economics. This also results in an integrated theory in which the market works regardless of the number of firms, meaning that there is no need for separate economic theories for monopoly, duopoly, oligopoly, etc, and perfect competition.

Most importantly, this reformation gives the traditional price theory correctness, consistency, completeness and self-efficiency, at a time that it has lost those features and has been reduced to only being complementary to the modern trends and methodologies in economics (game theory, decision theory, behavioral economics, empirical economics, experimental economics etc), as Weyl (2015) emphasizes. Thus price theory in its traditional form can regain its prestige and dominant position within economics.

# APPENDIX A:  The Fallacy around the Horizontal Demand Curve for the Firm

Antoine Augustin Cournot (1838) is the first economist who tried to indicate in a clear, definite and mathematical way the until then -and for many years later- indefinite concept of perfect competition ("unlimited competition" according to him). Being both a mathematician and an economist and examining the equilibrium in every type of market, starting from monopoly and duopoly and reaching perfect competition, Cournot utilized mathematical tools and based his theory on concrete and distinct principles and specifically the principle of profit maximization for each firm, i.e. this very same principle which was later used by marginalists and mainstream economics. In this way, he reached the well-known mathematical condition of profit maximization (using his original symbols):

$$D_k + [p - \Phi'_\kappa(D_k)]dD/dp = 0 \ ^8 \qquad \text{where}$$

$D_k$ is the production quantity of the producer "k" (the symbol D, instead of the usual q, is apparently used to connect production with the corresponding demand).

$p$ is the equilibrium price of the commodity's market.

$\Phi'_\kappa(D_k)$ is the marginal production cost of the producer "k" (expressed as derivative of the "cost–produced quantity" function $\Phi_\kappa(D_k)$.

$dD/dp$ is the derivative of the "total demand –price" function (slope of the total demand).

Starting Chapter VIII "Of Unlimited Competition", Cournot states:

*"The effects of competition have reached their limit, when each of the partial production $D_k$ is inappreciable, not only with reference to the total production $D=F(p)$, but also with reference to the derivative $F'(p)$, so that the partial production $D_k$ could be subtracted from D without any appreciable variation resulting in the price of the commodity. This hypothesis is the one which is*

---

[8] This equation is derived easily:

The profit of the producer is: $\qquad D_k \cdot p - \Phi_\kappa(D_k)$

By zeroing the derivative (with respect to p) of the above profit, for its maximization, we reach the said equation:

$D_k + p(dD_k/dp) - d\Phi_\kappa(D_k)/dp = D_k + p(dD_k/dp) - (d\Phi_\kappa(D_k)/dD_k) \cdot (dD_k/dp) = D_k + [p - \Phi'_\kappa(D_k)]dD_k/dp = 0$

and since, according to Cournot, $dD_k/dp = dD/dp$ (i.e. the slope of the individual demand curve for the firm equals that of total demand), the said equation is derived.

*realized, in social economy, for a multitude of products, and, among them, for the most important products. It introduces a great simplification into the calculations, and this chapter is meant to develop the consequences of it.*

*According to this hypothesis, in the equation*

$$D_k + [p - \Phi'_\kappa(D_k)]dD/dp = 0$$

*the term $D_k$ can be neglected without sensible error, which reduces the equation to* $\quad\quad p - \Phi'_\kappa(D_k) = 0$ *"* [9]

This excerpt, in my opinion, was going to lead the conventional theory to the fallacy about horizontal demand curve for the firms in perfect competition, in the following way:

The first sentence of the excerpt, according to which the production $D_k$ of each firm in perfect competition is so small compared to the total production (and demand) D that can be subtracted from (or added to) D without bringing about any appreciable variation to the product price, <u>was mistakenly interpreted as horizontal demand curve</u> for the individual firm's product, as according to the (wrong) interpretation of this phrase a firm can vary as much as it wants its production and sell at the equilibrium price without affecting this equilibrium price. There is no doubt that this interpetation is wrong, since Cournot himself considered in his theory the individual demand curve for the firm sloped with a slope equal to that of the total demand curve.

Any teaching handbook on Economics[10] but also many related research papers[11], draw upon that phrase in order to justify the horizontal demand curve for the individual firm which finally became prevalent in economics. E.g. Stigler (1957)[9] discussing about Cournot says:

*"How does revenue (say, pq) vary with output (q)? The natural answer is to*

---

[9] Cournot (1838) "Recherches sur les Principes Mathematiques de la Theorie des Richesses", New York: The Macmillan Conpany, ed. 1897, p.90.

[10] e.g. Ferguson (1969) "Microeconomic Theory", Richard D. Irwin Inc., 1969 (2nd ed.), Chapter 4, paragraph 4.5c.

[11] e.g. Friedman (1953) "The Methodology of Positive Economics" in *Essays on Positive Economics* (re-edited 1966), chapter 1, p.35, Chicago: University of Chicago Press. Stigler (1957) "Perfect Competition, Historically Contemplated", *The Journal of Political Economy*, February1957, Volume LXV, Number 1, pp 1-17, pages 5, 10.

*define competition as that situation in which p does not vary with q - in which the demand curve facing the firm is horizontal. This is precisely what Cournot did:*

**'The effects of competition have reached their limit, when each of the partial production $D_k$ is inappreciable, not only with reference to the total production D=F(p), but also with reference to the derivative F'(p), so that the partial production $D_k$ could be subtracted from D without any appreciable variation resulting in the price of the commodity.' ''**

However, the aforementioned phrase does not mean that the individual demand curve for the firm is a horizontal line, as it will be explained below:

With this misinterpreted phrase, Cournot wanted to denote the stability of the equilibrium price in perfect competition, which is reached -according to his view- when the competitive producers become so many and therefore the production of each producer so small, compared to the total demand, that a variation in this individual production (or the entry/exit of a single producer in/from the market) doesn't anymore change the equilibrium price (while until then it did change the price, as was the case when, for example, an additional producer was added to the 2, 10, or 100 incumbent producers) (see <u>Figure 1</u>).

However, all of the above don't actually mean that the individual demand curve for the firm is a horizontal line. For, of course **<u>after</u>** the equilibrium all firms will definitely become price takers and will comply with the result of equilibrium brought about by the competition between them; since **after** reaching equilibrium, the price in the market is one and the same,  even in oligopoly and even in duopoly (given that we talk about a homogeneous product and not a differentiated one), without this implying that the individual demand curve for the firm became a horizontal line. Because, **after** the moment that the stable equilibrium price prevailed in the market with the numerous firms of perfect competition and this price becomes known to both sides of the market (consumers and producers), it is apparent that the consumers will demand (and find) the product at this price, while the producers will illusively consider their individual demand curve a horizontal line, since they don't need to reduce this price to increase their sales and if they set a higher price they would sell nothing.

Yet, that this means a horizontal demand curve for the firm is totally misleading and based on misinterpreted arguments, for it does not refer to the real demand forces, that is the consumers' preferences, but to a superficial, ostensible and illusive quasi-demand state which is the result of the market equilibrium (that is the single price resulted from the equilibrium established for all the transactions **after** equilibrium) and not the root cause of this equilibrium. Because demand, at both the aggregate and firm level, is something that exists **before** the market equilibrium and is formed by the consumers' preferences, which remain unchanged after equilibrium. Besides, the price taking assumption is mistaken because we cannot take the equilibrium price as given, while we search to determine this price in equilibrium; that is to say, to take the equilibrium price after equilibrium, while we are before equilibrium.

The point is therefore not the price taking, which obviously prevails **after the equilibrium** in all the types of a homogeneous product market, but **how the equilibrium is determined beforehand**, i.e. what are the forces that beforehand lead to the equilibrium (what is the price maker). And these are no others than the forces of demand and supply, which, of course, remain the same before and after the equilibrium with no change in their curves' inclination, meaning that a sloping demand curve can not be horizontal at the time of equilibrium. Conventional theory perceives the total market demand as sloping (correct), but instead of distributing this total demand to the competing firms as it is logical and reasonable (due to indifference of consumers in the choice of the seller of the homogeneous product), it takes a horizontal individual demand for the firm, while still considering sloping the aggregate total demand (which, though, should be the sum of the individual firms' demands for each price).

Cournot himself, whose misinterpreted phrase led to all this fallacy about the horizontal individual demand curve in the economic theory, does not consider, as mentioned previously, the individual demand curves for the firms horizontal lines but, on the contrary, sloped and as a matter of fact having the slope of the total demand curve. But the mistake of Cournot was primarily this slope and position of the individual demand curve, as mentioned in Section 3. Because the choice of a producer to produce a specific quantity does not entail that this choice reduced the residual demand for the rest of the producers by this constant quantity for every price of the product; that is, that the residual demand for the rest of the producers was cut down for every price by the quantity that the first producer decided to produce. Simply because the production of a quantity by a producer does not imply that the consumers will buy all this quantity by him and they will not buy a part from other producers, given the homogeneity of the product. So, the "best response concept" of Cournot is wrong and the same stands also for the subsequent Nash game theory which is based on that Cournot concept.

The second mistake of Cournot was his perception about vast number of tiny firms for price stability in perfect competion. Cournot connected equilibrium stability with infinite number of tiny firms, so that each of them be not able to influence the total quantity and hence the equilibrium price. However, for stability it is not necessary the infinite number of tiny firms, but just the maximization of profit of firms, which takes place in only one and single point. Any movement away from this point reduces the maximum profit and for this reason the movement is not actualized by any firm, which provides the stability of equilibrium. Of course, this maximum profit becomes zero in perfect competition, due to the continuous entry of new firms (we always speak about the economic profit above the normal one). Cournot also concluded zero profit in perfect competition, but due to the infinite number of firms and their tiny size, which is unnecessary, because the profit becomes zero when the number of firms reaches a level where the ever decreasing revenue due to the entry of new firms equals the cost. Unfortunatcly, the Cournot's mistake about equilibrium stability did not stop there, but it was continued by the post Cournot neoclassicals with a worse confusion, since they misinterpreted the previous stability condition of Cournot as a horizontal demand curve for the firm (price taking principle). The big irony here is how they interpreted Cournot this way, since Cournot himself considered the individual demand for the firm as sloped.

Marshall (1890) also refers to the particular demand curve of the individual producer's own special market, which for him is generally very steep:
*"This may be expressed by saying that when we are considering an individual producer, we must couple his supply curve -not with the general demand curve for his commodity in a wide market, but- with the particular demand curve of his own special market. And this particular demand curve will generally be very steep; perhaps as steep as his own supply curve is likely to be, even when an increased output will give him an important increase of internal economies."*[12]

---

[12]  Marshall (1890) "Principles of Economics", 8th edition (1920), Macmillan and Co. Ltd, London, p 458 n1. See also pp 374, 458-59.

Stigler (1957), as a proponent of the price taking principle in line with the Chicago school, criticizes Marshall for this and for his resistance to be in line with the theory of his contemporaries:

*"Marshall as usual refused to float on the tide of theory, and his treatment of competition was much closer to Adam Smith's than to that of his contemporaries. ......................................we must remember that he discussed the "fear of spoiling the market" and the firms with negatively sloping demand curves in the main chapters on competition[41] and that the only time perfect competition was mentioned was when it was expressly spurned.[42]*

*Soon he yielded a bit to the trend toward refinement of the concept. Beginning with the third (1895) edition, he explicitly introduced the horizontal demand curve for the individual firm as the normal case and gave it the same mathematical formulation as did Cournot.[43] But these were patchwork revisions, and they were not carried over into the many passages where looser concepts of competition had been employed"[13]*

However, from a careful study of the Marshall's book on the above cited (under n.43) passage, it doesn't appear that Marshall "explicitly" introduced the horizontal demand curve for the individual firm, as Stigler states, but only that he adopted the Cournot's principle that the equilibrium price is not disturbed by a variation in the production of an individual producer in perfect competition where firms are numerous and of relatively small size; but apparently, Stigler considered that principle equivalent to the horizontal individual demand curve, as mentioned previously (p. 30). Besides, it is well-known that the whole Chicago school emphasized the price taking concept (Weyl, 2015).

One additional reason that most probably eased the way for the adoption of the horizontal individual demand fallacy is the second paragraph of the aforementioned Cournot's excerpt:

*"According to this hypothesis, in the equation*

$$D_k + [p - \Phi'_\kappa(D_k)]dD/dp = 0$$

*the term $D_k$ can be neglected without sensible error, which reduces the equation to* $\qquad p - \Phi'_\kappa(D_k) = 0$ *".*

---

[13] Stigler (1957) "Perfect Competition, Historically Contemplated", *The Journal of Political Economy*, February 1957, Volume LXV, Number 1, pp 9-10.

This phrase denotes that in perfect competition, since $D_k$, i.e. the individual production of each firm, is negligible, the equilibrium price equals the marginal cost of the firm. On the other hand, for profit maximization must *marginal cost = marginal revenue*. This results in price being also equal to the marginal revenue of the firm. This property (i.e. p=MR) does always happen if the demand curve of the firm is a horizontal straight line, which, most probably, strengthened the fallacy about the horizontal individual demand. To this property of the horizontal demand curve (p=MR=MC) is Stigler (1957) referring when, while discussing about Cournot, he states:

*"This definition of competition* (where $D_k \rightarrow 0$) *was especially appropriate in Cournot's system because, according to his theory of oligopoly, the excess of price over marginal cost approached zero as the number of like producers became large. .................. A market departed from unlimited competition to the extent that price exceeded the marginal cost of the firm, and the difference approached zero as the number of rivals approached infinity."*[14]

Further down Stigler (1957), discussing about Edgeworth, says:

*"It is intuitively plausible that with infinite numbers all monopoly power (and indeterminacy) will vanish, and Edgeworth essentially postulates rather than proves this. But a simple demonstration, in case of sellers of equal size, would amount only to showing that*

*Marginal revenue=Price + Price/Number of sellers x Market elasticity*

*and that this last term goes to zero as the number of sellers increases indefinitely.*[31] *This was implicitly Cournot's argument."*[15]
(in the related footnote 31, Stigler proves the above formula, which is equivalent to the Cournot's relevant one).

However, here seems to be the additional misinterpretation concerning the equality of price to the marginal cost and the marginal revenue of the firm in perfect competition, if this equality is attributed to a horizontal demand curve for the firm by the post-Cournot economists (as it seems to be attributed). Because in the Cournot system, the equality of price to the marginal cost and the marginal

---

[14] Stigler (1957) ibid p.5.

[15] Stigler (1957) ibid p.8.

revenue of the firm (which indeed holds in the Cournot perfect competition) is not due to a horizontal demand curve of the firm (on the contrary, the demand curve of the firm according to Cournot has the slope of the total demand), but due to the fact that this sloping individual demand curve has been moved to such a position in perfect competition (see <u>Figure 3</u>) that its peak on the price-axis (which is the only point where price equals marginal revenue) tends to coincide with the marginal cost value on this axis (even in case that the marginal cost is not constant as in Figure 3)[16].

Most of the other economists who significantly contributed to the development of the neoclassical theory of perfect competition[17] don't refer or avoid to refer to the issue of horizontal individual demand curve for the firm, at least up to/including (to the best of my knowledge) Knight (1921)'s book, which is considered to have completed the main aspects of the perfect competition theory. Whenever they referred to the equilibrium price, they usually referred only to the total demand curve of the market. However, the notion of price taking and horizontal demand curve for the individual firm was implicit in their thinking and this concept was later explicitly emphasized by the Chicago school (Weyl, 2015). Anyway, the important thing is that the horizontal individual demand curve fallacy has been developed, spread and eventually prevailed in the neoclassical and later in the mainstream economics.

The models of Chamberlin (1933) and Robinson (1933) resemble those of my approach, but the big difference is that those models referred to monopolistic and imperfect competition with similar but not exactly the same products, while the present consideration refers to pure perfect competition with a single homogeneous product, for which it proves that it has an inevitable monopolistic character.

Keen and Russell (2010) detected that the neoclassical theory of perfect competition does not maximize the aggregate profit of the industry, but they do

---

[16] The individual demand curve for the firm and its equilibrium point lie anyway (according to Cournot) very close to the price-axis due to the tiny size of each firm.

[17] e.g. Jevons (1871), Walras (1874), Edgeworth (1881), Fisher (1892), Pareto (1896), Clark (1899), Moore (1905), Pigou (1912, 1920), Knight (1921).
For a brief and comprehensive retrospect, refer to the paper of Stigler (1957) "Perfect Competition, Historically Contemplated", *The Journal of Political Economy*, February 1957, Volume LXV, Number 1, pp 1-17.

not identify the real individual demand curves for the firms, to develop a new revised theory. However, the present work was made in complete ignorance of even this element of their work.

## APPENDIX B:  The New Approach

This Appendix examines how the new approach works in the determination of the equilibrium both at firm and at market level (B.1), how equilibrium is reestablished after a market disturbance (for example, after a change in demand) (B.2) and compares equilibrium analyses at firm and at market level (B.3).

### *B.1. Equilibrium Process*

We examine first the equilibrium process according to this new approach both at firm and at market level (see Figure 10).

Let LAC be the long-term average cost curve of the typical enterprise of an industry and dd' the demand curve the enterprise faces in the short run (without perfect competition for the time being), which for simplicity is displayed graphically as a straight line. Let also the enterprise size have short-term average cost curve SAC' and short-term marginal cost curve SMC'. The equilibrium of the enterprise maximizing its profit will be attained at the production level where the marginal revenue of the firm, mr', equates its marginal cost, SMC', which corresponds to the point **e'** with price **p'** and production quantity **q'**. In this state of interim equilibrium an economic profit of **e'c'** per product unit is obtained, which will stimulate new firms to enter the industry, with the aftereffect of reduction of the individual demand for each firm and hence the rotation of its demand curve around its peak on the price-axis downwards[18]. The entry of new firms will continue until their economic profit will be completely eliminated due to competition, which is reached when the individual demand curve rotates downwards until it becomes tangential[19] (dd") to the short-term average cost curve SAC' at the point **e"** with equilibrium price **p"** and quantity **q"** (short-term equilibrium). However, due to the economic profit **e"c"** that still exists in relation to the long-term average cost LAC, the entry of new firms will continue, with a concurrent change in the size of all the firms, until their economic profit will be

---

[18] This rotation after the entry of new firms into the market is due to the equal distribution of the same total demand among more firms. This equal distribution implies that the peak of the total demand curve on the price-axis (demand=0) is also the peak price of the individual demand curves, and thus the centre of the rotation. This rotation is the critical distinction between this theory and the shift of the demand curve of the Cournot theory.

[19] See Appendix C: "Mathematical Validation" Section C.2.

49

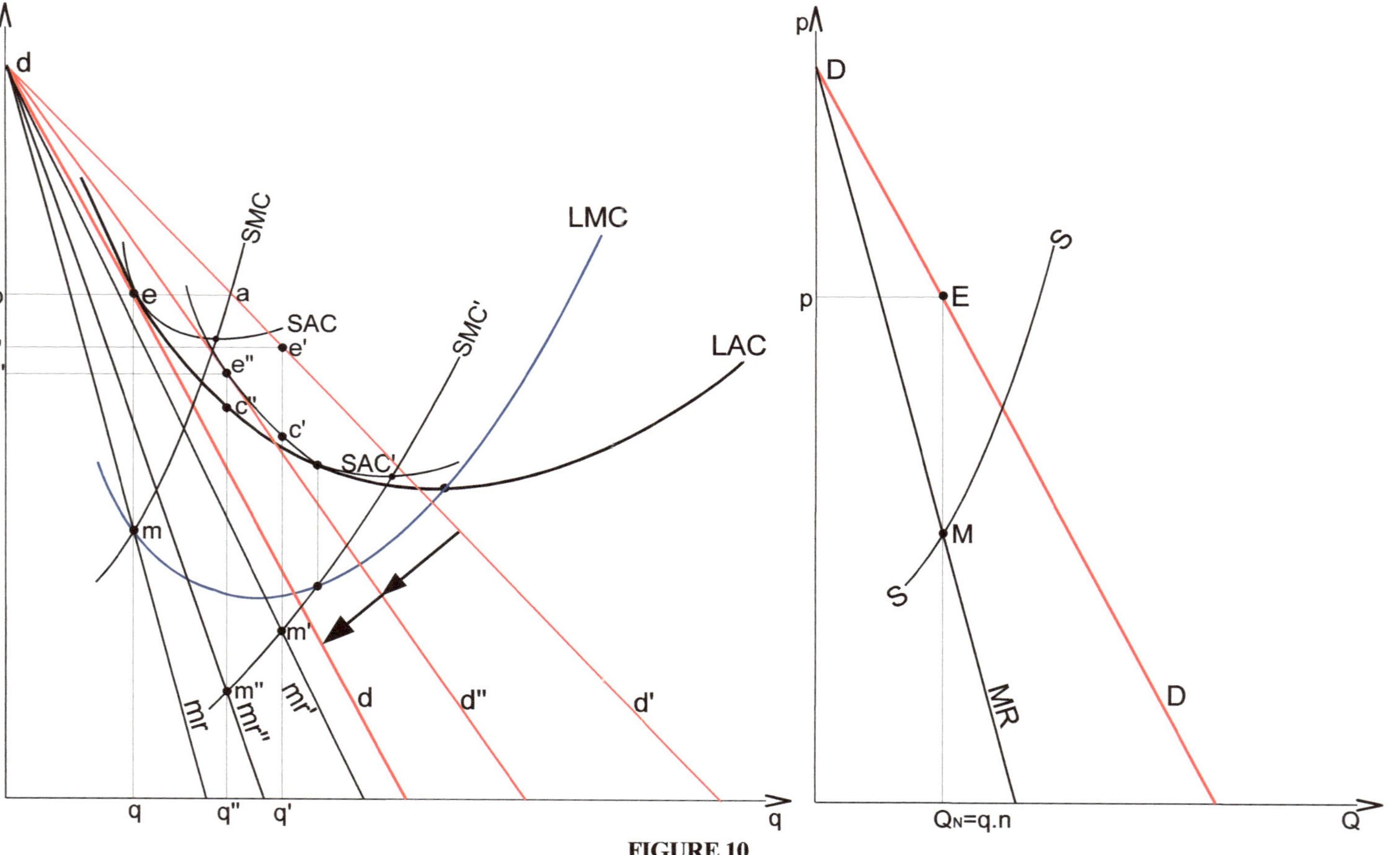


**FIGURE 10**

**Equilibrium Process at firm and at market level according to the new approach**

50

completely eliminated in the long run due to competition, which is reached when the individual demand curve rotates downwards until it becomes tangential[19] (dd) to the long-term average cost curve LAC at the point **e** with equilibrium price **p** and quantity **q**. This osculation point of the individual demand curve dd with the long-term average cost curve LAC is the long-term equilibrium point of the firm and implies the long-run adjustment of the enterprise size, so that the average cost curve (SAC) for the final size to also osculate LAC at this long-term equilibrium point **e**. It is proved[20] that this point of long-term equilibrium corresponds also to the intersection **m** of the marginal revenue curve mr of the long-term demand dd with the marginal cost SMC of the long-run adjusted enterprise size. That is to say, it is a point of profit maximization, but the economic profit in this state of long-term equilibrium is zero, as expected, because of the perfect competition and the free entry of companies into the industry (or exit if a loss is recorded). As it is known, the long-term marginal cost curve LMC goes also through this intersection point of the mr and SMC curves[21], since we refer to a long-term equilibrium at **e**.

We can determine the final number of firms (N) at the perfect competition state from their initial number (n) by the relation:

$$N = n \cdot (pa)/(pe) = n \cdot (pa)/q$$

At market level, the final long-term equilibrium is also presented in <u>Figure 10</u>, in the right side, for comparison to the firm's level. The total demand curve DD of the market, which is the sum of the individual demand curves for the firms of the industry, has the same shape as the individual demand curve of the firms, and as a matter of fact it is exactly the same as the individual demand curve of the typical enterprise, with the only difference that it corresponds to multiple quantities for the same prices, with multiplier of course the number of firms. The total supply curve SS of the market, which is the horizontal sum of the individual supply curves of the firms, has the same shape as the individual supply curve of the firms (which is the marginal cost curve) and is again exactly the same as the individual supply curve of the typical enterprise (SMC), with the only difference that it now corresponds to multiple quantities for the same prices, with multiplier

---

[20] See Appendix C.2 "Mathematical Validation".

[21] See Appendix C.2 "Mathematical Validation".

again the number of firms. The long-term equilibrium in the market, which maximizes the profit of the industry from the total demand, corresponds to the intersection of the total marginal revenue MR derived from the total demand curve DD, with the total marginal cost, that is the total supply curve SS, and takes place at the point **E**, with price **p**, the same as the price of the typical firm's long-term equilibrium, and quantity $Q_N$, a multiple of the typical firm's long-term equilibrium quantity scaled by the number of firms. The number of firms (**N**) in the long-term equilibrium of the market can be determined, given the total demand of the market DD and the individual demand of the typical firm dd, as the ratio of the quantities of the above two curves corresponding to any price p:

$$N=Q/q.$$

Therefore, the intersection of total supply SS and total demand DD, which according to the neoclassical theory of perfect competition is the equilibrium point of the market, does not maximize the total profit of the industry or, to put it differently, that intersection does not fully exploit, from the side of the industry, the total demand curve DD of the market; therefore, it cannot constitute the equilibrium point of the market. Because, since each firm maximizes its profit, the industry, as sum of the firms, should also maximize[22] the profit that derives from the total demand at the equilibrium state.


## *B.2. Change in Demand*

If a change takes place in the total demand, e.g an increase in the demand for the product, with a concurrent change in its slope (to make the case more general), then the new equilibrium will be reached as follows (see <u>Figure 11</u>):

Suppose the long-term equilibrium before the increase in demand lies on the point **e**, with individual demand dd and SAC curves both tangential to the LAC curve on this point and equilibrium price **p** and quantity **q**. The increase of the total demand funneled to the firms of the sector will result in a commensurate increase in the individual demand for the typical firm from dd to d'd'. An interim equilibrium will take place first at the intersection **m'** of the marginal cost SMC of the typical firm with the marginal revenue mr' of the new increased demand d'd', which corresponds to the point **e'** and to interim equilibrium price **p'** and

---

[22] See Appendix C.1 "Mathematical Validation".

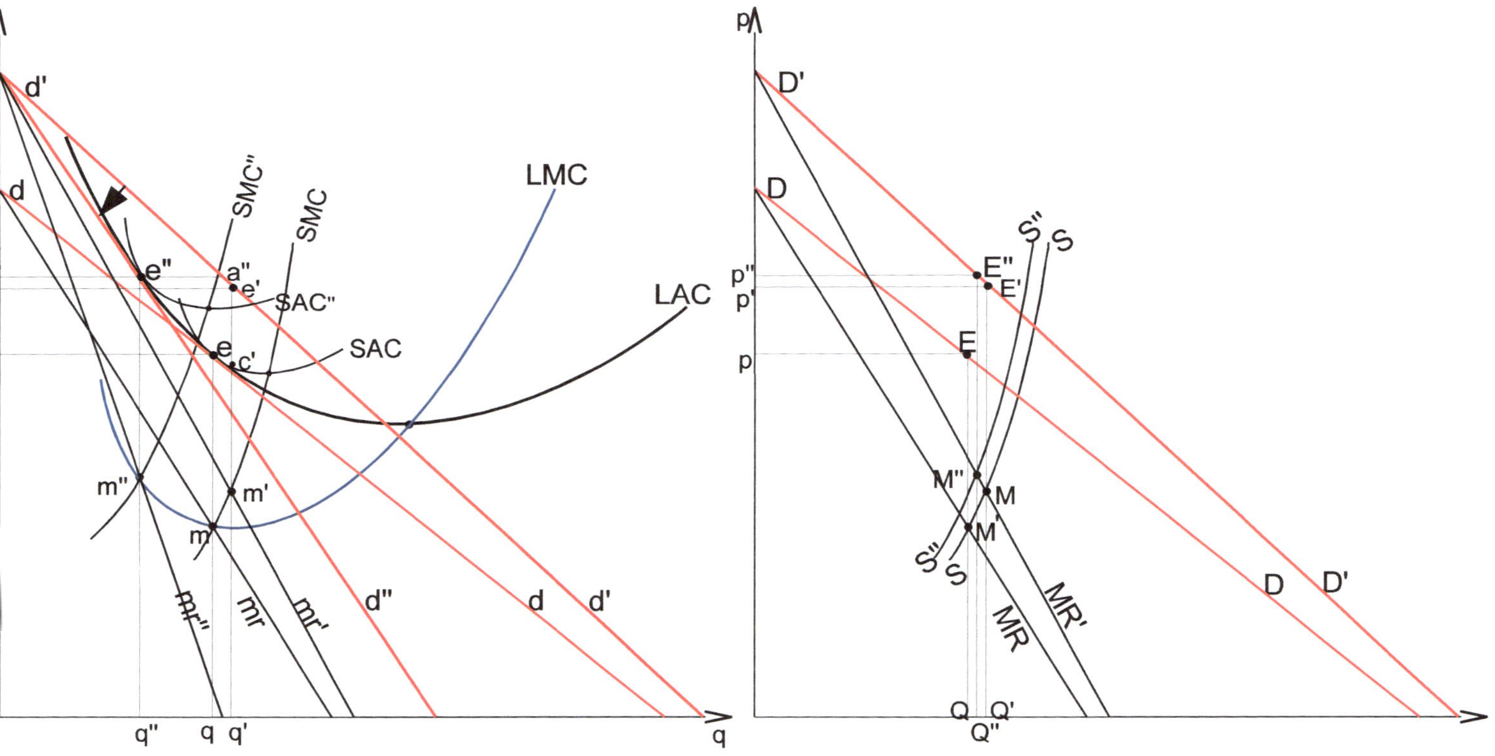


**FIGURE 11**

**Equilibrium at firm and at market level after a change in demand**

53

production level **q'**. This will generate an economic profit of **e'c'** above the normal, per product unit, which will cause the entry of new firms into the industry. Consequently, the individual demand of each firm will be reduced and the individual demand curve will gradually rotate around its peak on the price-axis downwards to the final position d'd", tangential to LAC at e", leading to disappearance of the extra profit and to a new long-term equilibrium. This final long-term equilibrium at **e"**, with equilibrium price **p"** and production level **q"**, is connected with a smaller size of the enterprise (from SAC and SMC to SAC" and SMC") and corresponds also to the intersection **m"** of the new marginal cost SMC" with the marginal revenue mr" of the final individual demand d'd" (as well as with the LMC curve, as it refers to a long-term equilibrium).

At market level, starting from the initial long-term equilibrium at **E**, the interim equilibrium after the increase in demand (from DD to D'D') will take place at the intersection **M'** of the total marginal cost SS (total supply curve) with the total marginal revenue MR' of the new increased demand D'D', which corresponds to the point **E'** and to  interim equilibrium price **p'** (the same as the interim equilibrium price of the typical firm) and quantity **Q'** (equal to the interim equilibrium quantity of the  typical firm **q'** times the  initial  number  of firms in the industry), while the number of firms will remain for the moment the same (**n**). It follows the entry of new firms into the market caused by the economic profit e'c' and the gradual rotation downwards of the individual demand curve from the position d'd' to its final one d'd", tangential to LAC at e", while the total market demand curve remains the same at its position D'D'[18]. The new long-term equilibrium is eventually established at the intersection **M"** of the new total marginal cost S"S" (total supply curve) with the total marginal revenue MR' of the increased total demand curve D'D', which corresponds to the point **E"** and to long-term equilibrium price **p"** (the same as the long-term equilibrium price of the typical firm) and quantity **Q"**.

The total number of firms at the new long-term equilibrium will be:

$$N = n \cdot (p''a'')/(p''e'') \quad \text{and also} \quad N = Q''/q''$$

where **n** is the number of firms at the initial long-term equilibrium.
The number of new entrants will be:

$$N\text{-}n = n \cdot (e''a'')/(p''e'')$$

### *B.3.  Firm Level v. Market Level Analysis*

The preceding analysis makes obvious that the crucial role in the determination of the market equilibrium and price lies at the firm level, where both the cost and the representative individual demand curve are formed -elements necessary and sufficient to determine the equilibrium state- and it doesn't lie at the market level, by means of the intersection of total supply and total demand, which in addition, as already explained, does not determine the equilibrium in the market.

Essentially, when we talk about market equilibrium, we mean the profit maximizing equilibrium of each firm (beyond that of consumers of course). As we have previously seen, this automatically implies the profit maximizing equilibrium at the aggregate market too. So, the transition from the firm to the market level, and vice versa, leads to consistent results, no matter where one starts examining the equilibrium from. Up to now, though, when we talked about market equilibrium, we usually meant the equilibrium in the total (aggregated) values (demand-supply) of the market, since at that level was where the single price -dominating every firm- was determined and where the examination of the equilibrium started from.

## C.1.  *Industry's Profit Maximization from Total Demand*

Let's assume an industry with "n" firms, with each firm "i" having:
individual demand   $q_i = q_i(p)$,   which under reverse form becomes   $p_i = p_i(q)$
and individual cost   $C_i = C_i(q)$.
The revenue of the firm is   $R_i = p_i(q)q$
and its marginal revenue:   $MR_i = dR_i/dq = p_i'(q)q + p_i(q)$
which under reverse form can be written (considering that MRi takes p values):

$$q_i = MR_i(p).$$

The marginal cost of the firm is   $MC_i = C_i'(q)$
and under reverse form it can be written (considering that MCi takes p values):

$$q_i = MC_i(p)$$

which denotes the quantity supplied by each firm given the price.

The equilibrium for each firm "i" is achieved at the quantity level $q_i$ where its profit is maximized, that is where its marginal revenue equals its marginal cost:

$$MR_i(p) = MC_i(p).$$

This however implies (by adding the equations) that for the aggregated values of the market will also be:   $\Sigma\, MR_i(p) = \Sigma\, MC_i(p)$

In the last equation, the left part equals the marginal revenue of the total market demand, since each $MR_i$ is the marginal revenue of each individual demand, while the right part is the sum of marginal costs of all the firms, which forms the total (aggregated) supply of the market. Both functions are in their reverse form, i.e. they provide quantities for a given price, and precisely speaking sums of quantities corresponding to the total demand and the total supply, respectively, of the market. This is the reason why the functions are taken reversed, so as to sum quantities for a given price or cost.

This last equation of the sums implies actually that the equilibrium of each firm results -at market level- in the equation of the total marginal cost of the market (total supply) with the total marginal revenue of the market coming from the total demand (and not with the total demand itself as the conventional theory states). Consequently, the equilibrium of the market (meaning the individual equilibrium of each firm maximizing its profit) automatically maximizes also the aggregate profit of the industry that comes from the total demand (taking into account the cost that comes from the total supply).

### *C.2. Equilibrium of the Firm*

Suppose the demand curve for the firm is: $\quad$ **p=p(q)**

The total revenue of the firm will then be: $\quad$ **R(q)=p(q)q**

and the marginal revenue of the firm will be $\quad$ **MR=dR/dq=p'(q)q+p(q)**

Suppose the average cost of the firm is: $\quad$ **c=c(q)**

The total cost of the firm will then be: $\quad$ **C(q)=c(q)q**

Therefore the marginal cost can be written as $\quad$ **MC=dC/dq=c'(q)q+c(q)**

The equilibrium takes place when **MR=MC** (profit maximization condition):

$$\mathbf{p'(q)q+p(q) = c'(q)q+c(q)}$$

In perfect competition, however, <u>both in the short and in the long run</u>, because of the free entry of firms due to profits (or exit due to losses), the economic profit (i.e. the profit beyond the normal one) becomes zero; hence the price equates the average cost (including the normal profit), i.e. **p(q₀)=c(q₀)** at the equilibrium point, and the previous maximization condition becomes:

$$\mathbf{p'(q_0)q_0 = c'(q_0)q_0 \quad or \quad p'(q_0) = c'(q_0)}$$

The above final condition demonstrates (see <u>Figure 9</u>) that the three curves -i.e. the average cost curves (SAC and LAC) and the demand curve (dd)- have the same tangent, that is they osculate each other at the point of equilibrium, where the economic profit is maximized but at the same time is zero (beyond the normal business profit) due to the perfect competition.

It is implied, of course, that in the long-term equilibrium the size of the enterprise has been adjusted so that to give final SAC curve osculating the LAC curve at the above point of long-term equilibrium. This implies that in the long-term equilibrium the three curves dd, LAC, SAC osculate each other at the same point (see <u>Figures 9, 10, 11</u>), where they have the same tangent:

$$\mathbf{p'(q_o) = c'_{LAC}(q_o) = c'_{SAC}(q_o)}$$

By multiplying by $q_o$, and as at the equilibrium osculation point: $p(q_o)=c_{LAC}(q_o)=c_{SAC}(q_o)$, it is concluded that:

$$\mathbf{p'(q_o)q_o+p(q_o)=c'_{LAC}(q_o)q_o+c_{LAC}(q_o)=c'_{SAC}(q_o)q_o+c_{SAC}(q_o)}$$

which means that:

$$\mathbf{MR(q_o) = LMC(q_o) = SMC(q_o)}$$

That is to say, the curves MR, LMC, SMC have the same value at the production level $q_o$ that corresponds to the point of long-term equilibrium and of osculation of the three curves dd, LAC, SAC. Consequently the curves MR, LMC, SMC intersect each other at the same point vertically below the point of long-term equilibrium and of osculation of the three curves dd, LAC, SAC (see Figures 9, 10, 11).

# References


**Cassels, J. M.** 1936. "Excess Capacity and Monopolistic Competition" *Quarterly Journal of Economics* vol.51 p.426-43.

**Chamberlin, Edward H.** 1933. "The Theory of Monopolistic Competition" Cambridge, Mass.: Harvard University Press.

**Clark, John Bates.** 1899. "The Distribution of Wealth: A Theory of Wages, Interest and Profits" New York: The Macmillan Company.

**Cournot, Antoine Augustin.** 1838. "Recherches sur les Principes Mathematiques de la Theorie des Richesses" Paris, New York: The Macmillan Company (1897).

**Edgeworth, Francis Ysidro.** 1881. "Mathematical Psychics" London.

**Ferguson, C. E.** 1956. "A Social Concept of Excess Capacity" *Metroeconomica* vol.8 p.84-93.

**Ferguson, C. E.** 1969. "Microeconomic Theory" Homewood, IL: Richard D. Irwin Inc. (2$^{nd}$ edition).

**Fisher, Irving.** 1892. "Mathematical Investigations in the Theory of Value and Prices" Yale University.

**Friedman, Milton.** (1953). "The Methodology of Positive Economics" in *Essays on Positive Economics* (re-edited 1966), chapter 1, p.3-43, Chicago: University of Chicago Press.

**Harrod, R. F.** 1934. "Doctrines of Imperfect Competition" *Quarterly Journal of Economics* vol.49 p.442-70.

**Jevons, William Stanley.** 1871. "The Theory of Political Economy" London: Macmillan & Co.

**Kahn, R. F.** 1935. "Some Notes on Ideal Output" *Economic Journal* vol.45 p.1-35.

**Keen, Steve, and Russell Standish.** 2010. "Debunking the Theory of the Firm – a Chronology" *Real-World Economics Review,* issue 53 p.56-94.

**Knight, Frank H.** 1921. "Risk, Uncertainty and Profit" New York, London School Reprints of Scarce Works, No 16 (1933).

**Marshall, Alfred.** 1920 (8th Edition). "Principles of Economics" London: Macmillan & Co. Ltd.

**Moore, Henry.** 1905. "Paradoxes of Competition" *Quarterly Journal of Economics* vol.20 p.209-30.

**Nomidis, Dimitrios.** 2015a. "A Reconsideration of the Theory of Perfect Competition" *Social Science Research Network (SSRN)* http://ssrn.com/abstract=2594577

**Nomidis, Dimitrios.** 2015b."Labor Market: Monopolistic Exploitation by Companies and Employees" *Social Science Research Network (SSRN)* http://ssrn.com/abstract=2599205

**Nomidis, Dimitrios.** 2016a. "The Fallacy of the Perfect Competition Theory" *Social Science Research Network (SSRN)* http://ssrn.com/abstract=2736690

**Nomidis, Dimitrios.** 2016b. "A Revision of the Theory of Perfect Competition and of Value" *Social Science Research Network (SSRN)* http://ssrn.com/abstract=2875582

**Pareto, Vilfredo.** 1896. "Cours d' Economie Politique", Lausanne.

**Pigou, Arthur Cecil.** 1912. "Wealth and Welfare". 1920. "The Economics of Welfare" London: Macmillan & Co. Ltd.

**Robinson, Joan.** 1933. "The Economics of Imperfect Competition" London: Macmillan & Co, Ltd.

**Stigler, George J.** 1957. "Perfect Competition, Historically Contemplated" *Journal of Political Economy* vol.65 p.1-17.

**Walras, Leon.** 1874. "Elements d' Economie Politique Pure, ou Theorie de la Richesse Sociale" Lausanne-Paris.

**Weil, Glen E.** 2015. "Price Theory" *Journal of Economic Literature* vol.53 No.3.

www.ingramcontent.com/pod-product-compliance
Lightning Source LLC
Chambersburg PA
CBHW040858110726
48005CB00001B/107